Kate 2022

Thought of you so

Enjoy!

Grandma Judy

BEYOND
CANNING

Quarto is the authority on a wide range of topics.

Quarto educates, entertains and enriches the lives of our readers—enthusiasts and lovers of hands-on living.

www.quartoknows.com

First published in 2016 by Voyageur Press, an imprint of Quarto Publishing Group USA Inc., 400 First Avenue North, Suite 400, Minneapolis, MN 55401 USA.
Telephone: (612) 344-8100 Fax: (612) 344-8692

quartoknows.com
Visit our blogs at quartoknows.com

Voyageur Press titles are also available at discounts in bulk quantity for industrial or sales-promotional use. For details contact the Special Sales Manager at Quarto Publishing Group USA Inc., 400 First Avenue North, Suite 400, Minneapolis, MN 55401 USA.

10 9 8 7 6 5 4 3 2 1

ISBN: 978-0-7603-4865-9

Library of Congress Cataloging-in-Publication Data

Giles, Autumn, 1984- author.
  Beyond canning : new techniques, ingredients, and flavors to preserve, pickle, and ferment like never before / Autumn Giles.
    pages cm
  ISBN 978-0-7603-4865-9 (paperback)
  1. Canning and preserving. 2. Pickled foods. I. Title.
  TX601.G465 2016
  641.4'2--dc23
                                        2015031835

Acquiring Editor: Thom O'Hearn
Project Manager: Caitlin Fultz
Art Director: Cindy Samargia Laun
Book Design and Layout: Amy Sly
Illustrator: Paul Tunis

Printed in China

BEYOND CANNING

NEW TECHNIQUES, INGREDIENTS, AND FLAVORS
to Preserve, Pickle, and Ferment Like Never Before

AUTUMN GILES

Voyageur
Press

CONTENTS

FERMENTATION 122

INTRODUCTION

My boyfriend and I learned quickly that when you buy a really old house in a really small town, everyone has a story about it. When word got out that we had purchased our first home, a bright pink, 110-year-old folk Victorian on our town's main drag, we were instantly inundated with "pink house" tales: "Did you know it used to be yellow?" "Geronimo made tortillas on the porch," and, my personal favorite, "I was married in your guest house because it used to be a chapel."

Before we even closed on our home, a friend of ours passed along a multipage, photocopied newspaper biography of Hattie, the woman who, in the early 1900s, raised eight children in our home, spoke many languages, and—most importantly to me—filled the cellar off the kitchen with home-canned food, which she subsequently gave away to those in need around town. After I learned Hattie was a preserver like me, I knew we had found *our* house, and I felt so proud to be stocking the cellar again.

There's a perception that preserving has "come back" in recent years, and perhaps among twenty-something urban dwellers, as I was when I first became interested in preserving, it has gained a greater following. However, between Hattie's time and mine, it hasn't *really* gone anywhere. In the same way that it made sense for Hattie to put up her surplus each year, preserving still makes sense to a growing number of people who are looking to source more of their food locally year-round and maintain a connection with traditional food ways. It remains an essential tool for those looking to cut back on food costs without compromising on quality and taste.

My favorite way to illustrate the economics of preserving is to talk about preserved lemons, the dead-easy yet completely transformative preserve made from salt, lemons, and time. Can I cook without preserved lemons? Absolutely. Indeed, I did for many, many years. However, in the depths of winter, do they infinitely improve my go-to roasted carrots? Without a doubt. I had never had them until I made them myself, because store-bought preserved lemons are cost prohibitive for me. Put simply, preserving empowers me to eat better for less.

In that spirit, I have written this book for those who have been putting up for years and are looking for their new favorite thing to do with plums and also for those who have more recently caught the canning bug and are ready to move beyond strawberry jam. Focusing on the three methods of preserving that I use most in my home kitchen—water-bath canning for sweet preserves, preserving with vinegar, and fermentation—this book will move beyond the basics, providing unique, contemporary, and safe small-batch recipes.

Finally, there is much to be said for the social and community-building aspects of preserving. The first time I canned was years ago during a canning party at a friend's apartment. Today I maintain many of the connections with fellow preservation enthusiasts that I made during that single afternoon. The joy that comes from honoring the harvest by gathering friends and family to put up food and share knowledge and stories is perhaps the greatest argument for preserving food. I can only hope that in a hundred years, the person living in my house hears a story about me filling up the cellar and feels at home, just as I did with Hattie.

HOME COOKS VERSUS PRESERVERS

My secret mission in writing this book, which is indeed now not so secret, is to get more folks to see themselves as preservers. I think many of us, myself included for a long time, see the work of preserving as something separate from cooking. There are home cooks—plenty of them—and then there are preservers. At its best, I think preserving is just another, albeit invaluable, tool for the home cook's toolbox. If you obsess over

making the perfect fried egg, then why not also make the perfect kraut to go alongside it? Particularly as the excitement around eating locally and seasonally continues to grow, I argue that passionate home cooks can become better at what they love by having the skills to preserve. For more seasoned preservers, this can look like further integrating their practices as preservers and home cooks, which is always a goal of mine.

Especially in recent years, as preserving has gained even more mainstream appeal, I think the general perception of what sort of person cans (or ferments or infuses) has shifted. To put it simply, preserving isn't *only* putting up all the food your family will eat throughout the winter. It certainly can be that, but it can also be smaller projects for the savvy home cook that make the most of what's on hand—a generous friend with a productive lemon tree or the third week in a row of CSA turnips. For me, a huge part of becoming a more experienced preserver was not only learning what I liked but also learning which preserved foods were most useful to me as a home cook and which ones gave me the most pleasure to

prepare and to eat. Build and refine your preserving practice around those two cornerstones: pleasure and practicality.

WHY IT WORKS AND HOW TO MAKE SURE IT WORKS IN YOUR KITCHEN

Since this book is organized by technique, processes and equipment specific to each technique will be covered at the beginning of each section. However, it's worth addressing general questions about safety here, particularly since we're talking about growing the ranks of preservers, and safety concerns can be perhaps the most significant barrier to preserving. There are questions specific to each of the techniques covered in the book—sweet preserves, preserving with vinegar, and fermentation—so I'll address them separately.

I love the assurance that Kevin West gives in *Saving the Season* that if you can safely cook chicken, then you're capable of preserving food at home. Yes, just as the USDA has developed a set of best practices for

WHAT TO MAKE WHEN

There aren't any asparagus recipes in this book; I did that on purpose. After a long winter, I am so darn happy to see asparagus, that the last thing I want to do is preserve it. I just want to eat it—immediately and often. There have been times when I've been so excited to preserve something that I haven't taken the time to enjoy it. This may go without saying, but the first week you see something at the greenmarket for the season, it's best to buy a little and savor it, rather than buy a lot and preserve it. I know from experience that this can be a hard thing. However, prices will be significantly higher when a fruit or vegetable is early in its season, and the quality is not likely to be at its peak.

In her first book, *The Hip Girl's Guide to Homemaking*, fellow preserver and DIY maven Kate Payne recommends keeping a kitchen journal. I think this is a great tip, especially when it comes to preserving. I use my journal to keep track of my recipes: when I made them, what price I bought the produce for, how much I made, and if I made any tweaks to a recipe. Take stock of any leftover preserves in your larder as the beginning of the new preserving season approaches and note that as well, as it will help you adjust what you make for the coming year. For example, if you still have last season's peach butter around and peaches are coming back in season, consider making less in the future. Keep track of the recipes that are keepers and those that aren't. Over time, this journal will become an incredible catalog of your preserving knowledge. Beyond just showing you how far you've come, it will help you make more of what you love and less of what you don't.

Keep a kitchen journal.

the safe handling and preparation of chicken, it also maintains a set of standards for how to safely preserve foods. Although safety should be taken seriously, it should also be kept in perspective. We have rules for cooking chicken and we have rules for making preserves, and folks have been doing both successfully and safely for a very, very long time.

That said, it's important to understand what makes a recipe safe, so you can avoid inadvertently doing something that makes it unsafe. Sweet preserves deal mostly with high-acid fruits—in the preserving world that is anything with a pH lower than 4.6. This means they can be processed safely in a water-bath canner. There are exceptions—including figs and tomatoes, for example, in the recipes that follow—that must be acidified using bottled lemon juice, which has a more standard acidity than fresh lemons, to be safely processed in a water-bath canner. It is important to follow recipe directions from a trusted source, use bottled lemon juice when indicated, not add or subtract ingredients, and process for the indicated amount of time, adjusting for altitude as needed. Basically, follow a recipe from a trusted source and follow it to the letter, unless it indicates otherwise.

In doing so, you'll ensure a high-acid environment where the botulinum bacterium—which secretes the botulinum toxin, responsible for the rare but potentially deadly food-borne illness botulism—cannot grow. I think that's worth repeating: botulinum cannot grow in a high-acid environment. If you've followed a trusted recipe and something goes wrong in a sweet-preserve recipe, it will be very apparent. You'll notice carbonation, mold, a popped lid, an alcoholic smell, or evidence that the jar has leaked after storage. These sorts of things are incredibly rare but are worth noting so that you know to discard any jars that exhibit these characteristics.

Vinegar-based preserves that are processed in a water-bath canner also rely on acidity to make them work and keep them safe. Although many pickles start with low-acid vegetables like cauliflower, they are made safe for water-bath canning with a high-acid vinegar brine. Unless otherwise noted, you must use a vinegar that has been diluted to 5 percent acidity, which will be indicated on the label.

With vinegar-based preserves, as with sweet preserves that are processed in a water bath, it is important to follow recipe directions from a trusted source; do not reduce or replace the vinegar nor add or subtract ingredients, and process for the indicated amount of time, adjusting for altitude as needed. In addition, acetic acid, the main acid in vinegar, evaporates quicker than water, so cooking a vinegar-based preserve for far longer than indicated can throw off your pH and should be avoided. Again, follow a recipe from a trusted source. If you have done so and something goes wrong, it will be immediately noticeable in the form of carbonation, mold, a popped lid, an alcoholic smell, or evidence that the jar has leaked after storage. Toss anything that looks or smells off.

Fermentation is quite a different beast, but ultimately similar in that it, too, relies on acid to preserve.

Unlike the pickling process, for example, acid isn't added at the onset; the lactic acid produced by bacterial fermentation preserves the food and inhibits the growth of spoilers. In order to create a safe and successful final product when you're fermenting, it is important to observe standards regarding the amount of added salt. For dry-salted recipes (more on that later, but basically kimchis, krauts, and everything in between), calculate 1.5 to 2 percent of the total weight of the produce you're using after it is prepped, and add that much salt by weight. To create a brine to safely ferment vegetables, calculate 5 percent of the *weight* of the water you'll use and add that much salt by weight. Introducing the proper amount of salt into a ferment encourages lactic acid bacteria (that's good) and creates an inhospitable environment for bacteria that cause spoilage (also good).

Another important safety element in lacto-fermentation is creating an anaerobic environment—no oxygen—to keep the anaerobic lactic acid bacteria working their best to preserve the food. This is why it's important to keep vegetables submerged below the brine. When bits of veggies poke above the brine and are exposed to oxygen, spoilage happens. Using an airlock to allow carbon dioxide to escape during the fermentation process, without letting oxygen in, as I do in the small-batch recipes that follow, in effect expands the anaerobic area to include everything below the airlock. This means you can be a bit less meticulous when it comes to keeping things submerged below the brine at all times. That said, it is important to understand how the process works in general, particularly if you go on to use a crock for larger batches or decide that airlocks aren't for you.

Within those parameters, in the realm of lacto-fermentation, we're less tied to recipes than we are with water-bath canning. It is safe to experiment with a variety of vegetables using these standard salt ratios. More on how to do that successfully, that is, how to end up with something delicious, later.

SWEET
PRESERVES

THE FIRST THING MOST PEOPLE THINK of when they hear the word "canning" is jam. I might even be so bold as to say that the first thing that comes to mind is strawberry jam. Jam is iconic, and yet there's a reason that this chapter is called "sweet preserves" and not "jams"; there aren't really that many classic jam recipes in the pages that follow. Let me explain.

Jams in the traditional sense, in the way they're often historically referred to and replicated in American preserving literature, include a mixture of sugar and chopped or mashed fruit, cooked to a stiff gel set at 221°F. Now, there's nothing inherently wrong with making jam this way. In fact, I made plenty of these sorts of jams in the early years of my canning, but—frankly—I learned that I don't really like them.

As I became more and more interested in food preservation, I also became increasingly fanatical about produce. I suspect if you're holding this book in your hands, then perhaps you can relate to feeling giddy about black raspberries and kind of freaking out about fresh bergamot. I began to think of preserving, as it relates to sweet preserves, in a broader sense. I was interested in not only literally preserving the food so that it was shelf stable but in preserving the character of the fruit as much as possible—its shape, fresh taste, scent, and texture.

I found this was best done in smaller batches of relatively low-sugar, no-added-pectin preserves, which often include a maceration period and do not result in a firm set—and aren't meant to. With some worthy exceptions, those are the sorts of preserves you'll find here. I figure if I'm lucky enough to come by the miracle that is unsprayed sour cherries, I ought to honor them by preserving not only the fruit itself, but also its character.

THE FRUIT

When possible, use organic, unsprayed, or backyard fruit. This is especially important with preserves in which the peel is cooked, such as marmalade. Did I only use organic fruit to test the recipes in this book? No. Did I choose organic and unsprayed whenever I could? Absolutely.

For organic, unsprayed fruit that grows off the ground—and therefore is not as likely to contain grit—a visual inspection for bugs and other debris can take the place of washing, especially if it comes from a trusted source. I wash organic store-bought produce but wouldn't worry about washing something from a U-pick that I knew was unsprayed and grew off the ground. Don't wash your fruit until you're just about to use it, and gently remove excess water from the fruit before proceeding with the recipe.

In an ideal world, you'd pick the fruit off the tree and preserve it the same day. Quite idyllic, right? For those of us for whom this isn't possible, there are a few ways to keep your fruit in tiptop shape from the time it comes into your life until it goes into jars. First, choose shallower containers, or for things like peaches and large tomatoes, lay them out, stem end down, on a flat surface. In a bowl full of ripe fruit, the fruit on the bottom of the bowl is under a lot of weight and more likely to bruise and become damaged. Placing fruit in as shallow a container as possible prevents this. I like to leave the fruit out of the fridge as long as I can, simply because I enjoy looking at it and smelling it when I walk by, but also because it's easier to spread out fruit outside the fridge than inside. When the fruit reaches its peak of ripeness and it's time to move it into the fridge, do so on something like a rimmed cookie sheet, if possible.

Another way to prolong the period between procurement and preserving is maceration. Maceration, which I'll talk about later in much more detail as it relates to specific recipes, is just a fancy way of saying toss the fruit with some sugar. Many of the recipes that follow have a maceration period built in, which can both buy you some time and break up the process into increments that can be stretched over a longer period, like a few nights after work. Recipes that call for an overnight maceration period won't be ruined if they end up macerating for two days, but I wouldn't go much longer than that if you can help it. Because maceration sucks the juices out of the fruit, macerating for too long is like taking too long a bath: you'll end up with shriveled fruit, and the final texture of your preserve will suffer.

I'd be remiss if I didn't mention the ultimate procrastination method—or time-buying strategy if I'm being polite—when it comes to sweet preserves: freezing. Say you went a little overboard at the farmers' market and maybe didn't need that extra two pounds of rhubarb when you already had a pound in the fridge, and there's just no way you're going to get to it this week. Freeze it. Frozen fruit makes beautiful preserves and has inspired some of my most favorite cross-seasonal fruit combinations (like the Grapefruit-Rhubarb Preserves on page 34). My basic method for freezing fruit when my eyes are bigger than my preserving docket is wash, dry, cut/pit/peel if necessary, and spread on a parchment-lined baking sheet in the freezer. Once the fruit is frozen, transfer to resealable plastic freezer bag.

Finally, and this almost goes without saying, choose the highest-quality produce you can. Fruit with surface bruising can be salvaged by removing the bruised portion, but quite overripe or deeply bruised fruit should not be used for preserving.

THE SUGAR

I rarely use plain old white sugar in my kitchen, but I make an exception for preserves, and I'm going to urge you to do the same. Although it's refined and often vilified (not without reason), white sugar has its place. Here's why: Sugar serves to enhance the flavor and texture of a preserve, but the sweetener in a preserve should not have a distinguishable flavor—unless it's intentional; instead, it should amplify what's already there. Making your preserves with refined white sugar will allow the taste and appearance of the fruit to shine through cleanly. Organic cane sugar, which I often prefer to use in cooking and baking, contains both additional moisture and additional flavor. Will it ruin your preserves if you use it? No. But you will probably taste the difference. Also, for those of us who eat with our eyes, know that organic cane sugar will muddy the final color of the finished product. Furthermore, additional moisture is the enemy of preserves because, in general, we're looking to cook the liquid out of the fruit as quickly as possible—again, for the benefit of taste and texture.

I never thought I'd be in a position to make a case for granulated white sugar, but here it is. When a recipe in this book refers to sugar, it means refined white granulated sugar, unless specified. If you're looking to explore low- or no-sugar preserves, there are great books out there specific to those topics.

THE STUFF

It's a misconception that there's a lot of special equipment required for putting sweet preserves in jars. Though, yes, you will need **jars**. When I refer to jars in the following recipes, I mean those sold under the brands Kerr and Ball in the United States, with a two-piece lid-and-band closure. There's an initial investment when it comes to jars, but you'll have them for just short of forever. The jars themselves you can reuse until they begin to exhibit cracks or chips, which hopefully won't happen very frequently. Every new flat of jars you buy will come with lids and bands. The lids cannot be reused, but the bands can. Buy a packet of replacement lids (no bands) when you're ready for more. If you're anything like me, you'll soon find yourself with more bands than you know what to do with.

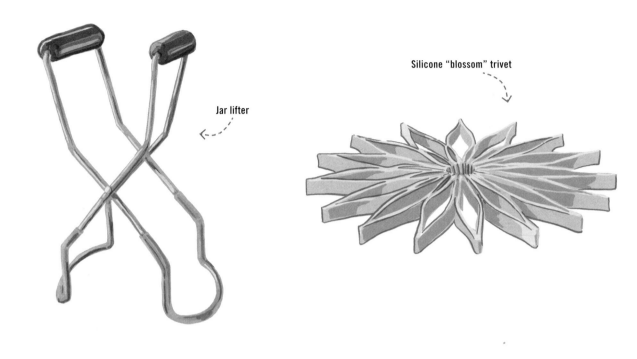

Jar lifter

Silicone "blossom" trivet

The big speckled canning pot used for processing jars, which is ubiquitous in hardware and grocery stores everywhere, is another one of the icons of preserving that I'm going to undercut. None of the recipes in this book require a pot like that, so don't go out and buy one until you're ready to put up a couple of boxes worth of tomatoes. All the recipes in this book can be processed in a **tall stockpot with a lid,** in which the water can cover the jars by at least 3 inches. Because we need to keep the jars off the bottom surface of the pot to prevent breakage, I use a **silicone "blossom" trivet**, a great recommendation by Marisa McClellan, creator of the website Food in Jars, which can be easily found on Amazon.

When you're actually ready to put the preserves into jars, there are few specialized pieces of equipment that are nonnegotiable but quite affordable. A **jar lifter** is one of them—because I don't want you sticking your hand in a pot of boiling water to grab a scalding hot jar! The jar lifter is what you'll use to take jars out of and put jars into the boiling water bath, and there's really no good substitute. Some folks use regular kitchen tongs, but I find them a bit unsteady. The other unitasker that is a necessity here is a **wide-mouth canning funnel**. This is simply a funnel that has a bottom opening as wide as a regular-mouth jar. It's a godsend when it comes to successfully steering hot, sticky preserves into jars.

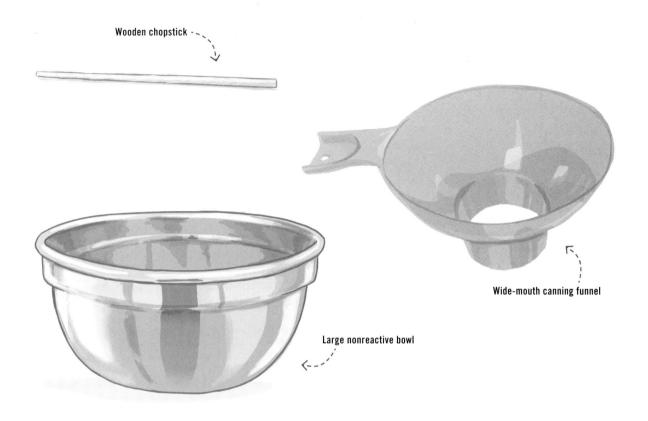

Wooden chopstick

Wide-mouth canning funnel

Large nonreactive bowl

I hope that most of the rest of the necessary items are things you may already have on hand. They include: a **wooden chopstick** for removing air bubbles from jars (metal can scratch), **paper towels** for wiping jar rims, a **clean kitchen towel** for placing hot jars on (they shouldn't go directly on the counter), a good **spatula** (I like the seamless silicone ones because they resist gunk), a **ladle**, and a heavy-bottom pot (as heavy as you have) for your **preserving pot**. For many of the recipes, in particular those that include a maceration period, a **large nonreactive bowl** will be necessary.

There are a few things that aren't necessary to begin canning but are nice to have and may be used for a handful of the recipes in this book. I think of these as "add-to-the-wish-list items," so when holidays and birthdays roll around you can make it as easy as possible for friends and family to enable your canning habit. These items include a food mill, an immersion blender, a jelly bag, a cutting board with a reservoir for cutting particularly juicy fruit, a cherry pitter, a strawberry huller, a food processor, and a good citrus zester/vegetable peeler. As you can see, it's easy for this list to get out of hand.

BASIC PRESERVING EQUIPMENT

You'll want to round up the following basic equipment before you get started putting preserves in jars:

- Half- or quarter-pint mason jars with two-piece lid closure
- Jar lifter
- Tall stockpot with a lid and silicone blossom trivet for processing
- Wooden chopstick
- Wide-mouth canning funnel
- Clean kitchen towel
- Paper towels
- Preserving pot
- Ladle
- Large nonreactive bowl

THE CASE FOR QUARTER-PINT JARS

Quarter-pint, or four-ounce jars, are the smallest jars available for water-bath canning. I know some folks find them a little fussy because they hold such a small amount (a scant half cup if we're getting technical), but for many sweet preserves, they're my absolute favorite. As hard as it is to believe, I'm pretty much the only jam eater in my two-person, two-cat household. Having multiple jars of jam open at one time, which is usually the case, starts to feel a little unmanageable when they all hold a cup. Plus, with smaller batch sizes like the ones in this book, processing the preserves in smaller jars means more jars to give away, without giving it all away! For any recipe where the yield is expressed in half pints, you may can the recipe in quarter-pint jars without adjusting the processing time. Canning whole fruit in syrup or a preserve with very large chunks makes less sense in quarter pint jars, but for many preserves, they're great.

FINDING YOUR PRESERVING POT

Initially, finding your preserving pot can be as easy as finding a reasonably sized nonreactive (stainless steel or enameled cast iron) pot. If you're someone who cooks with any frequency, this is likely something you already have. For small batches, a medium-size stainless steel pot, probably the one you use for pasta, will work well—the heavier the bottom, the better. Pans made with reactive substances like aluminum or cast iron will—not surprisingly—react with the acid in the fruit as you cook and can leave your preserves with a metallic taste. Choose the size of your pot

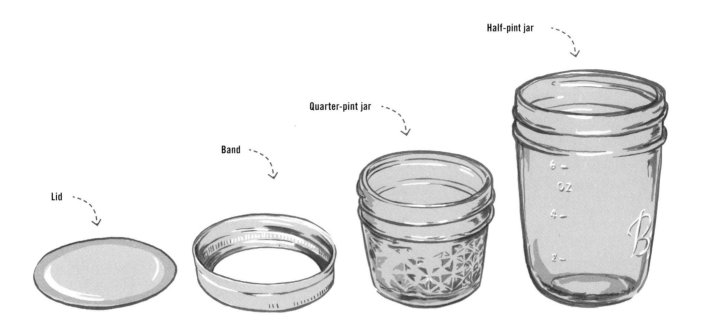

Lid

Band

Quarter-pint jar

Half-pint jar

by keeping in mind that when you start cooking, your pot shouldn't be more than one-third full.

In other words, you don't need to spend hundreds of dollars on a French copper jam pot, but I bet that it won't be long until you start coveting one. The shape of these pots is what makes them especially suited for jam making, so keep your eyes peeled for a pot of a similar shape that's a little more affordable. Look for something with a base that is smaller than the top, and sides that are slightly flared, in order to hack a fancy copper pot at a lower price.

Most importantly, though, you'll learn what you like as you preserve more and more, and hopefully you'll find a jam pot that feels like *yours*. I've relied on different jam pots over the years as my income and batch sizes have fluctuated. For most of the preserves in this chapter (save for the marmalades, which require something a little bigger) I use a wide, high-sided sauté pan, which works well because the larger surface area helps liquid cook off faster. I also like using a small enameled cast-iron dutch oven (this is good for the marmalades and larger batches) and know many others who use similar vessels for their jam making. It isn't flared, but it otherwise fits the bill.

SIMMERING LIDS

A lid wand—a short plastic stick with a magnet on the end, used to lift lids out of a simmering pot of water—used to be on the list of canning must-haves for the same reason as the jar lifter: the whole reaching-into-the-boiling-water thing. In August 2014, Jarden Home Brands, the folks behind Ball and Kerr jars, announced that it was no longer necessary to simmer their lids to help soften the sealing compound and create a steadfast seal. According to Jarden, "After many years of research, it was determined that preheating Ball and Kerr lids is no longer necessary. The sealing compound used for our home canning lids performs equally well at room temperature as it does preheated in simmering water (180°F). Simply wash lids in hot, soapy water, dry, and set aside until needed." If like me, you're in the habit of simmering lids before applying them, it won't hurt; just avoid overheating them—simmer, but don't boil.

THE PROCESS

I've always been a little lazy when it comes to *mise en place*, the French term that refers to getting all of a recipe's ingredients prepped and ready before starting the cooking process. Mise en place is what you see when you watch cooking shows and there are many tiny glass bowls filled with ingredients. While taking mise en place to that level can be a bit tedious, not to mention that it produces more dishes to wash, getting everything ready for water-bath processing before cooking a preserve is essential.

First, ready your water-bath canner for processing. Place a silicone trivet in the bottom and then add the jars, reserving the lids and bands. Always add more jars than you think you'll need. I do this part right on the stove so I don't have to move a stockpot full of water. Using a pitcher or tea kettle, pour the water into the stockpot, pouring it into the jars first so they don't float, then letting it fill around them. If you have hard water, you'll want to use filtered water. (If when you remove the jars from the water bath they're coated with a white powdery film, you have hard water. Empty the pot, wash the jars, and start over with filtered water.) Once the pot is full, cover it and bring it to a boil over high heat.

As your pot is coming to a boil, set out what you'll need for the processing. This includes clean lids and bands, a jar lifter, a wide-mouth canning funnel, a ladle, a chopstick, and a clean towel spread out enough to hold all the jars. I lay all these items out on the counter, cooking-show style, so they're ready when I need them. Then, I begin to cook the preserve.

Now, you do have to pay attention to timing as the jars need to be ready at the same time as the preserve, but nothing will be irrevocably ruined if things get a little off. When I cook rice for dinner I always start it first, knowing that it can sit off the heat with its lid on for a good amount of time after it is done cooking and it will stay warm. Same principle here—aim for the pot of water to have come to a boil well before the preserve is done. Once it has come to a boil, turn off the heat and remove the jars, leaving one or two in to help hold down the trivet, about 5 minutes before the preserve is done cooking. The ideal scenario is to have clean, dry jars when your preserves are ready.

So how do you know when your preserves are done? Of course, each of these recipes has a recommended cooking time, but inevitably it will vary in your home kitchen due to a number of factors, including the size and shape of your pan, moisture content of your fruit, and so on. I urge you to use the cooking times as a guide and develop your sense of when a preserve is done using visual and tactile clues. I grew up watching my mom gently press her finger into a cake to test its spring after it had been in the oven for the amount of time indicated in a recipe. We have those same sorts of tests for preserves, which in my experience are the most accurate indicators of doneness.

TIMER VERSUS STOPWATCH

So many of us, myself included, keep our devices close at hand in the kitchen. My phone has the sticky splatter marks to prove it. I would guess that many of you already use a phone timer when cooking, but I'm going to suggest changing things up just a bit when cooking preserves.

To time the processing period on your water-bath canner, you should absolutely use a timer because accuracy is important. However, when I'm cooking preserves, I use the stopwatch feature on my phone because it gives me an idea of how long the preserves have been cooking but forces me to stay engaged, check in, and stir the mixture frequently, which I should be doing anyway! That way, I'm paying attention to how the jam looks and feels and developing a sense of when it's done, rather than relying on a timer to tell me.

These visual cues tell you that your preserve is *really close* to being done. At this point, you should remove your jars from the water bath, remove your preserving pot from the heat, and test the preserve for doneness. Testing too early is better than overcooking a preserve, particularly when you're still getting the hang of knowing what a preserve looks and feels like when it's almost done:

- One of the classic tests for doneness is called "sheeting." It's a way to test preserves for doneness that is described as when a preserve moves off a lifted

THE SHEET TEST

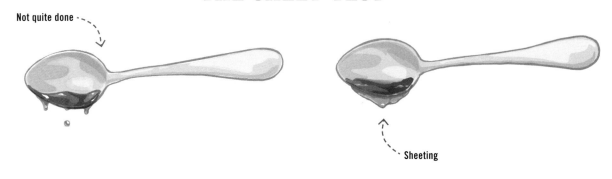

Not quite done

Sheeting

spatula in sheets, rather than drips. In my experience, this effect is much less dramatic than it sounds and can therefore be a bit misleading. Here's how I use this test to determine when a preserve is almost done: when you lift up your spatula, watch for individual drips to widen and slow before dripping, sometimes joining together before falling.

- Big, glassy bubbles are another visual cue that you're super close. At different points in the cooking process, the bubbles are small and sometimes foamy, but when a preserve is close to being done, the bubbles will get larger and glassier.

When you notice one or both of these "almost done" indicators, it's time to cut the heat to test the preserve for doneness. I prefer and recommend the plate test, because I find it the most simple and reliable, particularly for recipes like many of those in this chapter that aren't meant to reach a firm gel set. Here's how you do it: Once you have removed the preserve from the heat, place a small dollop on a saucer or small plate. Then place the plate in the freezer for a few minutes. This rapidly cools the preserve so that you can get a more accurate idea of the set. Remove the plate from the freezer and drag your finger through the middle of the dollop. It's done when it doesn't run back together. If it's not done, bring the preserve back to a boil and test again after a minute, once again removing it from the heat as you test for doneness. With marmalades and other higher-pectin preserves, you'll also notice that the preserve wrinkles when you begin to draw your finger through it.

This is the point at which you want your jars to be dry but still warm. If they're not dry, the hot preserves can sit for a few more minutes. Position your funnel over your jars and ladle in the hot preserves, leaving ¼-inch headspace (that's the space between the preserve and the top of the jar), unless otherwise indicated. Gently stir the preserve with a wooden chopstick, moving it around to help remove air bubbles. Wipe the rim of the jar with a clean, damp paper towel and drop a lid on top of each jar. If you have a lid wand, you can use that tool to help. Screw on the bands until they're fingertip tight, that is, just until you meet resistance. Place the full jars into the water bath in a single layer and confirm that they're covered by at least 3 inches of water. Cover the water bath and bring it to a full rolling boil over high heat. Begin your timer only once the pot has reached a full rolling boil.

Once the indicated processing time is up, remove the lid and let the jars sit for 5 minutes. Then, using the jar lifter, remove the jars from the water bath, placing them on the clean kitchen towel that you spread out earlier. Any water resting on the jar lids is fine; avoid tilting them to get the water off. At this point, you'll hear the pleasing ping of the jars sealing. Allow the jars to cool undisturbed for 24 hours. After 24 hours, check the seals by removing the bands and holding each jar by its lid. Label, date, and store out of direct sunlight without the band for up to a year. Refrigerate any jars that did not seal.

ALTITUDE

I currently live in Arizona at a little over 3,500 feet. When I started canning, I lived in New York City, more or less at sea level. I'm a creature of habit, which can be a good thing for remembering all the necessary steps of the canning process. On the flip side, it took me quite a while to get in the habit of making the necessary adjustments to my processing time for higher altitudes. The required adjustments to processing times in a water-bath canner for those at altitudes over 1,000 feet are as follows:

- 1,001–3,000 feet: increase processing time by 5 minutes
- 3,001–6,000 feet: increase processing time by 10 minutes
- 6,001–8,000 feet: increase processing time by 15 minutes
- 8,001–10,000 feet: increase processing time by 20 minutes

It's important to note as well that as you increase your processing time, more water will evaporate, so starting with ample water covering your jars is particularly important.

CRANBERRY, ORANGE & HAZELNUT conserve

A FESTIVE FALL CONSERVE WITH TERROIR

In the taxonomy of preserves, conserves are somewhere between jam, chutney, and marmalade. Like chutney, they often have dried fruits; unlike chutney, they also often have chopped nuts. Like a jam, they are a sweet preserve of sugar and fruit; and, like a marmalade, they often include citrus, peel and all! In other words, they're the best of all worlds.

A bit of a luxury, hazelnuts are a worthy splurge for this festive conserve. Rich and complex, creamy hazelnuts are sometimes compared to Chardonnay. This shared flavor affinity was the inspiration for this conserve, which marries cranberries and orange with Chardonnay and hazelnuts. Especially suited for a holiday cheese plate, this conserve pairs nicely with an Oregon blue cheese to honor the terroir of the hazelnuts—99 percent of the hazelnuts grown in the United States are grown in Oregon!

INGREDIENTS

1 orange
1 cup Chardonnay
¼ cup hazelnuts
1½ cups sugar
3 cups fresh cranberries, or 1 (12-ounce) package

MATERIALS

Basic supplies for sweet preserves (see page 18)
Fine mesh strainer
Parchment-lined baking sheet
Additional clean kitchen towel

Yield: about 2 half pints and 1 quarter pint

DAY ONE

1. Slice off the ends of the orange and place it on one of its flat ends. Using a sharp knife or vegetable peeler, remove the peel from the orange in strips about 1 inch wide, leaving behind as much white pith as possible.

2. Cut the strips crosswise to form very thin pieces of orange peel. Place in your preserving pot.

3. Cut the peeled orange in half and position a fine mesh strainer over the pot with the peels. Juice the orange into the fine mesh strainer, letting the juice combine with the peels. Discard the juiced orange.

4. Add the Chardonnay to the orange juice and peels. Bring the mixture to a boil over high heat, then reduce the heat to low and simmer for 5 minutes.

5. Let cool to room temperature, then refrigerate overnight.

DAY TWO

To prepare the hazelnuts:

1. Preheat the oven to 375°F.

2. Roast the hazelnuts on the parchment-lined baking sheet until the skins begin to blister, about 12 to 15 minutes.

3. Remove the hazelnuts from the oven and carefully wrap them in a clean towel and let stand for 1 minute to steam. (I find the easiest way to do this is to pick up the parchment and use that to transfer the nuts to the towel.)

4. After a minute, rub the hazelnuts inside the towel to remove the skins.

5. Once cool to the touch, use your hands to take the hazelnuts out of the towel, leaving the skins behind and rubbing off any stubborn skins with your fingers.

6. Set aside to cool completely.

To prepare the conserve:

1. Coarsely chop the hazelnuts and set aside.

2. Remove the orange-peel mixture from the fridge and add the sugar and the cranberries. Over high heat, bring to a boil that cannot be stirred down, then reduce heat to medium-high and cook for 5 minutes, stirring constantly.

3. Stir in the hazelnuts and cook for a minute more.

4. Although you can remove this from the heat and test for doneness using the plate test (see page 22), there's so much pectin in cranberries and orange peel that this will have no problem setting.

5. Ladle into prepared half- and quarter-pint jars, leaving ¼-inch headspace. Remove air bubbles and wipe rims. Place the lids on the jars and screw on the bands until they're fingertip tight.

6. Process in a water-bath canner for 15 minutes, adjusting for altitude as needed.

7. After 24 hours, check the seals. Label, date, and store out of direct sunlight without the bands for up to a year.

INGREDIENTS

1½ pounds (about 5 cups) blueberries

1½ cups sugar

2 tablespoons fresh-squeezed lemon juice

MATERIALS

Basic supplies for sweet preserves (see page 18)

Yield: about 3 half pints

blueberries
IN THEIR OWN
SYRUP

DAY ONE

1. Place the blueberries in a large nonreactive bowl. Take two handfuls of blueberries and smash them in your fists. The goal here is to keep most of the blueberries whole.

2. Add the sugar and lemon juice and use a spatula to toss. Let the mixture sit on the counter for 1 hour.

3. Refrigerate overnight.

DAY TWO

1. Transfer the blueberry mixture to your preserving pot.

2. Over high heat, cook until the bubbles begin to appear large and glassy, about 8 minutes.

3. Remove from heat and test for doneness using the plate test (see page 22). This preserve is done when you run your finger through a dollop of the cooled preserve, and it doesn't run back together.

4. Ladle into prepared half-pint jars, leaving ¼-inch headspace. Remove air bubbles and wipe the rims. Place the lids on the jars and screw on the bands until they are fingertip tight.

5. Process in a water-bath canner for 10 minutes, adjusting for altitude as needed.

6. After 24 hours, check the seals. Label, date, and store out of direct sunlight without the bands for up to a year.

THE BEST PANCAKE TOPPING AROUND

When I lived in New York, I saw any trip out of the city as an opportunity to hit up a U-pick operation in the vicinity. Could we pick apples on the way to a wedding and show up dirty, sweaty, and mosquito bitten to the rehearsal dinner? Yes, we could. What about picking peaches on a quick trip to Philly? Definitely!

In that spirit, there was no way I wasn't going to try to tack a fruit-picking trip onto a few nights in Vermont. I came home on the train with a box full of blueberries in my lap.

Back in my apartment, I attempted to coax the fragile blueberries into a preserve, suspending them in their own syrup. The results were just what I wanted. Thanks to a two-day cooking and maceration period, the blueberries mostly stayed whole, happily swimming in their own juices. Unless you have a good amount of underripe berries in the mix (and if you do, by all means use them), this will be a syrupy preserve—meaning it will not have a firm set. I see this as a boon, not a bust, as this makes the ideal pancake, waffle, and ice cream topping, yet still works like a charm on toast.

hot & sour CHERRY PRESERVES

A CHERRY PRESERVE WITH IMPECCABLE TEXTURE AND A KICK OF HEAT

Sour cherry preserves are on my short list of must-make preserves each season. Along with the first rhubarb of the year, sour cherries are one of the things that I get slightly fanatical about seeing on greenmarket tables. Smaller with a brighter, true-red color than their sweet cousins, sour cherries are at their best when cooked, not eaten out of hand. Although completely safe to eat raw, they're pretty puckery. Once cooked into a confection, or simply stewed, they possess the archetypal cherry flavor.

This recipe makes just 2 half pints (or 4 quarter pints if you're so inclined), so it's on the small side of small batch, because just as they're coveted, they can be a bit pricey. After pitting the cherries, toss them with sugar and refrigerate for an overnight maceration. A little kick of heat goes incredibly well with cherries, but if it's not your thing, you can omit the ground cayenne. The result is two preserves in one—a tart, rich cherry syrup and succulent stewed cherries.

INGREDIENTS

1½ pounds (about 4 cups) pitted sour cherries

1⅓ cups sugar

2 tablespoons fresh-squeezed lemon juice

¼ teaspoon cayenne

MATERIALS

Basic supplies for sweet preserves (see page 18)

Yield: about 2 half pints

DAY ONE

1. Gently stir together the pitted cherries, sugar, and lemon juice in a large nonreactive bowl.

2. Cover and let the mixture sit at room temperature for 1 hour, then cover and refrigerate overnight.

DAY TWO

1. Transfer the macerated fruit mixture to your preserving pot using a spatula to scrape any sugar that has settled to the bottom of the bowl.

2. Add the ground cayenne and, over high heat, bring the mixture to a boil that cannot be stirred down.

3. Continue to boil, stirring frequently until the mixture passes the plate test (see page 22), about 12 minutes. You can reduce the heat near the end of the cooking time if the mixture begins to scorch.

4. Ladle into prepared half-pint jars, leaving ¼-inch headspace. Remove air bubbles and wipe rims. Place the lids on the jars and screw on the bands until they are fingertip tight.

5. Process in a water-bath canner for 10 minutes, adjusting for altitude as needed.

6. After 24 hours, check the seals. Label, date, and store out of direct sunlight without the bands for up to a year.

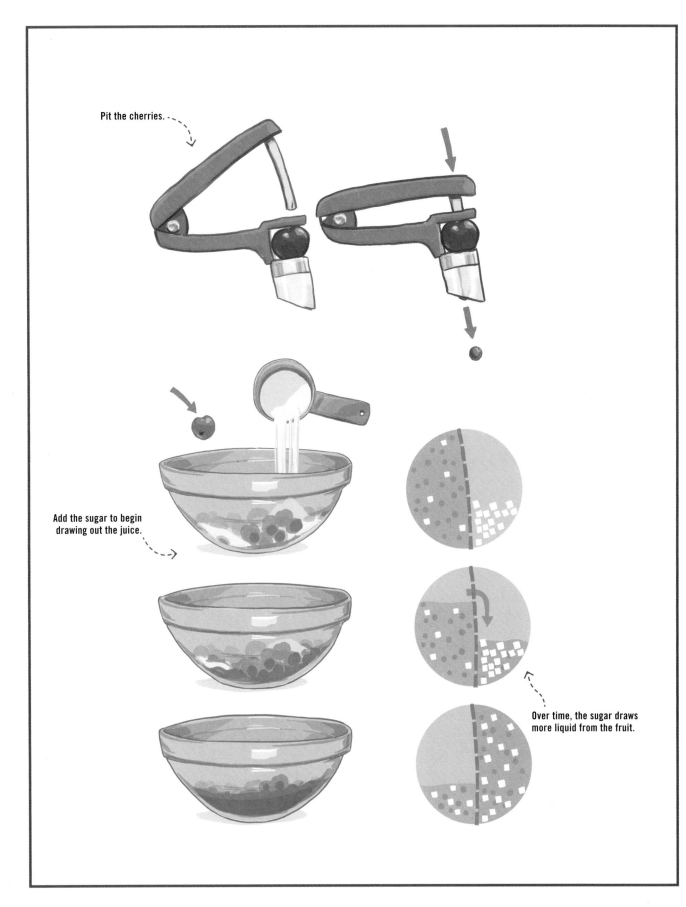

Pit the cherries.

Add the sugar to begin drawing out the juice.

Over time, the sugar draws more liquid from the fruit.

INGREDIENTS

28 ounces (about 5 cups)
red cherry tomatoes, halved

2 vanilla beans

1½ cups sugar

2 tablespoons bottled lemon juice

MATERIALS

Basic supplies for sweet preserves
(see page 18)

tomato-VANILLA JAM

Yield: about 2 half pints

DAY ONE

1. Halve the cherry tomatoes and place them in a large, nonreactive bowl.

2. Using a sharp knife, split the vanilla beans lengthwise and scrape out the seeds. Reserve the pods.

3. Place the sugar and vanilla bean seeds in a separate, smaller nonreactive bowl. Use your hands to rub the vanilla bean seeds into the sugar until all the large clumps of vanilla are broken up.

4. Stir the sugar and vanilla mixture gently into the cherry tomatoes along with the bottled lemon juice. Bottled lemon juice is required in this recipe to make it safe for water-bath processing. Tuck the vanilla bean pods into the fruit-sugar mixture so they are submerged, cover, and refrigerate overnight.

DAY TWO

1. Transfer the mixture to your preserving pot using a spatula to scrape any sugar that has settled to the bottom of the pan. It is normal for the tomatoes to have let out a lot of liquid.

2. Over high heat, bring the mixture to a boil that cannot be stirred down, stirring to help the sugar dissolve.

RECIPE CONTINUES ON PAGE 33

FEATURING AN UNLIKELY FLAVOR PAIRING INSPIRED BY JAM-MAKING LEGEND CHRISTINE FERBER

French pastry chef Christine Ferber has achieved somewhat of a cult following among preserving nerds, of whom I will proudly admit that I am one. Her jams and preserves, which only became available in the United States in recent years, use homemade apple pectin and seek to preserve the natural spirit of the fruit. There's no arguing that she continues to inspire preservers around the world. I certainly count myself among those who owe her a huge amount of credit.

In her book *Mes Confitures*, there is a recipe for tomato-vanilla jam. Here we're keeping the unexpected pairing—you're going to have to trust me on this one—and reworking the recipe so it's a little more accessible. The only prep work involved here is halving ripe cherry tomatoes and letting them settle in for an overnight maceration. As the preserve cooks, the tomatoes will naturally break down, resulting in a thick, jammy preserve.

3. Continue cooking the mixture on high until the jam passes the plate test (see page 22), about 15 minutes. Begin testing earlier if you see signs that the jam is almost done, and reduce the heat to medium-high if the jam shows signs of scorching, such as sticking and burning in spots. Remove from heat and discard the vanilla bean pods.

4. Ladle into prepared half-pint jars, leaving ¼-inch headspace. Remove air bubbles and wipe rims. Place the lids on the jars and screw on the bands until they're fingertip tight.

5. Process in a water-bath canner for 15 minutes, adjusting for altitude as needed.

6. After 24 hours, check the seals. Label, date, and store out of direct sunlight without the bands for up to a year.

MACERATION & MIDDLE SCHOOL SCIENCE

Christine Ferber's book brought maceration into my preserving practice, so it's only fitting to talk about it in depth here. In preserving, when we talk about maceration, we're talking about tossing cut or mashed fruit with sugar. Even if this is the first preserving book you've ever picked up, if you've tossed strawberries with sugar to spoon over crepes or waffles, you've used maceration to your culinary advantage.

Savvy preservers love maceration for two reasons. First, it draws the juices out of the fruit, creating a natural syrup. You remember learning about osmosis in middle school science class, right? That's what is happening here. Sugar is hydrophilic, which means it attracts water. In the case of sugar and fruit, the sugar attracts the liquid from inside the fruit's cell walls. The result is a syrup that is full of concentrated flavor that—after just a short time—will provide enough liquid to begin cooking the preserve without scorching. The end result is a beautiful preserve of fruit suspended in syrup.

Second, as food scientist Shirley Corriher told Saveur, the sugar is "also preserving the mixture of pectic substances that holds the cells together so that the fruit isn't reduced to mush." In other words, it sets the texture. This part of the maceration process is why the Hot & Sour Cherry Preserves on page 28 can only be described as toothsome. Maceration adds textural interest to the final product by partially preserving the original texture of the fruit. In the pages that follow, you'll notice that many of the recipes involve a maceration period. This is simply because I think maceration makes better preserves. On a practical level, though, I also appreciate the convenience built into splitting the work of a recipe over multiple days.

Grapefruit-RHUBARB PRESERVES

A CROSS-SEASONAL MARRIAGE OF TART FRUITS AND TEXTURE

I try to freeze at least a little rhubarb every year. I'm so excited to see it in the spring that my enthusiasm gets the best of me, and before I know it, I have 4 pounds of pink stalks poking out of my fridge. Later in the summer or fall (or winter, let's be honest), this results in some freezer clean-out preserves that span the seasons. This is exactly what happened here, and I'm so glad it did because I don't think these two unlikely tart fruit pals would have found their way together otherwise.

This recipe requires that you supreme the grapefruit (see page 36), which simply means cutting the citrus flesh away from the membranes. I will be the first to admit that I hated supreming for a really long time. It's a pain, it feels a little precious, and—most importantly—I was pretty bad at it. A couple of things changed to make me feel better about supreming. One was practice and the other, more important, factor was my knife. It *really* needs to be sharp. I'm not exaggerating when I say sharpen it right before you supreme. I just use my very unfancy at-home sharpener, and it still makes a huge difference.

INGREDIENTS

2 pounds (about 2 medium) red grapefruit

1 pound (about 4 cups) rhubarb, sliced ½ inch thick

2 cups sugar

MATERIALS

Basic supplies for sweet preserves (see page 18)

Cheesecloth or a scrap of white cotton tea towel

Yield: about 3 half pints

DAY ONE

1. Cut 1-inch-thick strips of peel from the grapefruit, leaving as much pith behind as possible.

2. Stack 3 or 4 pieces of peel together and julienne until you have ¼ cup of julienned peel. Add to the preserving pot.

3. Once you have enough peel, supreme the grapefruit (see illustration), reserving the seeds and as much juice as possible. I find the easiest way to catch as much juice as possible is to work over a bowl or Pyrex measuring cup. Squeeze the "rag" of the grapefruit, the membrane that remains after you have cut away all the fruit during supreming, to extract as much juice as possible. Measure 1½ cups supremed grapefruit sections and juice.

4. Tie the seeds up in a square of cheesecloth or scrap of white tea towel. Add them to the preserving pot with the julienned peel, grapefruit flesh and juice, rhubarb chunks, and sugar. Over high heat, bring the mixture to a boil that cannot be stirred down. Immediately remove from heat, let cool, and refrigerate overnight.

DAY TWO

1. Remove and squeeze the grapefruit seed packet into the preserving pot.

2. Over high heat, bring to a boil that cannot be stirred down. Reduce to medium-high and cook, stirring frequently, until it passes the plate test (see page 22). This small batch sets up quickly, in less than 10 minutes.

3. Ladle into prepared half-pint jars, leaving ¼-inch headspace. Remove air bubbles and wipe rims. Place the lids on the jars and screw on the bands until they are fingertip tight.

4. Process in a water-bath canner for 10 minutes, adjusting for altitude as needed.

5. After 24 hours, check the seals. Label, date, and store out of direct sunlight without the bands for up to a year.

SUPREMING CITRUS

INGREDIENTS

1½ pounds (about 4 medium) Meyer lemons

4 cups water

3½ cups sugar

2 tablespoons bergamot zest, grated finely using a microplane or similar grater (about 1 bergamot)

MATERIALS

Basic supplies for sweet preserves (see page 18)

Microplane or other fine grater

Cheesecloth or a scrap of white cotton tea towel

Yield: about 4 half pints

bergamot-SCENTED MEYER LEMON MARMALADE

A FINE-SHRED MARMALADE THAT'S WORTH THE FUSS

An unlikely marriage of the prim and proper—thin-skinned, mild Meyer lemon and the bold, heady bergamot—this marmalade became an instant favorite. I was inspired to create this marmalade because these two citrus fruits share a distinctly floral perfume, the Meyer's more delicate; the bergamot's much more assertive. Together, they're unexpectedly lovely.

Now, I prefer marmalades that are a little more labor intensive, but only because it's worth it. After making the three-day Fine-Shred Lime Marmalade from *Saving the Season* by Kevin West, I was a fine-shred convert. The result is a nearly translucent jelly with tender pieces of peel suspended within. This method cuts down on bitterness and chew in the final product, making it an ideal preserve for converting those who may be on the fence about marmalade.

Add the bergamot zest at the beginning of the cooking time for a more subtle bergamot flavor, or at the end for a more pronounced one. If you can't find fresh bergamot, simply omit it, but I promise it's worth tracking down.

DAY ONE

1. Slice off the ends of 1 lemon and place it on one of its flat ends. Using a sharp knife or vegetable peeler, remove the peel in strips about 1 inch wide. Leave behind as much white pith as possible. Repeat with the remaining lemons.

2. Use a sharp knife and then your fingers to peel off any extra pith or remaining patches of skin. Reserve the fruit.

3. Julienne the lemon peel very thin by stacking 3 or 4 pieces on top of one another and slicing them. Place the julienned lemon peel in your preserving pot and set aside.

4. Now, slice the reserved fruit in half lengthwise and slice the half lengthwise again. Cut each piece crosswise to form many small ⅛-inch-thick Meyer lemon triangles. Reserve the seeds as you go. Put the lemon slices in a medium-size nonreactive bowl as you work.

5. Once the lemon flesh is sliced, tie up the seeds in a square of cheesecloth or scrap of white tea towel. Add them to the preserving pot with the julienned peel and cover with the water.

6. Bring to a boil, reduce heat to low, and simmer for 5 minutes. Remove from heat and add the reserved fruit and any collected juices. Refrigerate overnight.

RECIPE CONTINUES ON PAGE 39

DAY TWO

1. Add the sugar and, for a less assertive bergamot flavor, the bergamot zest. (For a *more* assertive flavor, add it after the mixture has cooked for about 15 minutes.) Over high heat, bring to a boil that cannot be stirred down, stirring frequently. Cook until it passes the plate test (see page 22), about 18 minutes.

2. Ladle into prepared half-pint jars, leaving ¼-inch headspace. Remove air bubbles and wipe rims. Place the lids on the jars and screw on the bands until they are fingertip tight.

3. Process in a water-bath canner for 10 minutes, adjusting for altitude as needed.

4. After 24 hours, check the seals. Label, date, and store out of direct sunlight without the bands for up to a year.

WHAT TO DO IF YOUR CITRUS ISN'T ORGANIC

I had the crazy privilege of visiting a particularly expansive U-pick citrus orchard when I was working on this book—one of the perks of living in the desert! All the fruit was unsprayed and cheap, and the orchard had stuff I had never dreamed of seeing in person, including two bergamot trees. For a fruit fangirl like me, it was a pretty unreal experience.

Having spent my fair share of winters on the East Coast paying ungodly amounts of money for fancy citrus, I know this isn't the norm. It may be difficult to find any fresh bergamot, let alone organic. So, what do you do if your citrus isn't organic and you want to use the peel or zest? Conventional supermarket citrus can be treated with both fungicides and wax, so scrubbing thoroughly with hot water is recommended. Rinse and dry them thoroughly before using.

lavender APPLE BUTTER

INGREDIENTS

3 pounds apples, cored and cut into 1-inch chunks

1 cup water

6 tablespoons sugar

1 tablespoon fresh-squeezed lemon juice

½ teaspoon dried culinary lavender buds

MATERIALS

Basic supplies for sweet preserves (see page 18)

Food mill

Immersion blender

Yield: about 2 half pints

AN APPLE BUTTER THAT WORKS WITHOUT THE CINNAMON

I'm 100 percent in support of warming fall spices like cinnamon, nutmeg, ginger, and allspice. Now that I live in a place without leaves, I have to DIY my fall, and the kitchen is a great place to do it. Apples are often the beneficiaries of these autumnal spices, and apple butter is no exception. However, I think we do apples a disservice if we only think of them in the context of fall flavors. This apple butter, creamed with an immersion blender and cooked down until truly buttery, is studded with dried culinary lavender buds. Along with a bit of fresh lemon juice, the lavender brings out the bright, clean taste of the apples.

The amount of lavender in this recipe may not seem like much, but keep in mind that any whole spice that you leave in the jar, as we're doing here, will continue to impart its flavor after the jars are sealed and sitting in the larder. Plus, with lavender in general, a little goes a long way. A spoonful or two of this apple butter is my preferred companion for plain, whole-milk greek yogurt.

1. Bring the apples and water to a boil over high heat, stirring frequently as the apples begin to break down.

2. Reduce heat to medium-low and simmer until the apples are soft and can be broken apart easily with a spatula.

3. Let the mixture cool slightly, then process the apples and any remaining cooking liquid in a food mill. Position the food mill over a large bowl and process until only a dry pulp of peel remains. Discard the pulp.

4. While the mixture is still in the bowl, use an immersion blender to blend until very smooth.

5. Return the apple purée to your preserving pot, add the sugar, lemon juice, and lavender, and bring to a boil over high heat. Reduce heat to low and cook for 45 minutes to 1 hour, or until a dollop on a plate mounds and does not weep juice around the edges. Stir more frequently at the end of the cooking time and reduce the heat to low if necessary to prevent scorching.

6. Ladle into prepared half-pint jars, leaving ¼-inch headspace. Remove air bubbles and wipe rims. Place the lids on the jars and screw on the bands until they are fingertip tight.

7. Process in a water-bath canner for 10 minutes, adjusting for altitude as needed.

8. After 24 hours, check the seals. Label, date, and store out of direct sunlight without the bands for up to a year.

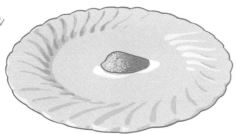

Weeping juice; not done.

Ready.

RANGPUR LIME *marmalade*

FEATURING AN ODDBALL CITRUS THAT'S SURE TO BECOME A NEW FAVORITE

One gray February day, an unexpected priority-mail box showed up at my apartment. This was miraculous for a couple of reasons. First, getting a package delivered successfully on the first try in New York City is the stuff of legends. Second, the box was full of Rangpur limes, the tart, musky cross between a mandarin orange and a lemon. My friend Shae is a bit of a backyard-grown citrus fairy, and I was so happy to be on her delivery list that year.

Rangpur limes look like small mandarin oranges. They're limes in name only. I fell so in love with their unique flavor that I was determined to grow some of my own, never mind that I lived in an apartment in a climate that was rather inhospitable to citrus. Our little fire escape Rangpur lime tree lasted longer than I ever thought it would. She gave me one little harvest of Rangpur limes before deciding she had had enough of this living-in-the-Northeast nonsense—just enough for a small batch of marmalade like this one.

INGREDIENTS

1½ pounds (about 5 large) Rangpur limes

4½ cups water

3½ cups sugar

MATERIALS

Basic supplies for sweet preserves (see page 18)

Cheesecloth or a scrap of white cotton tea towel

Yield: about 5 half pints

DAY ONE

1. Slice off the ends of one Rangpur lime and place it on one of its flat ends. Using a sharp knife or vegetable peeler, remove the peel in strips about 1 inch wide. Leave behind as much white pith as possible. Repeat with the remaining fruit.

2. Use a sharp knife to help peel off any extra pith or remaining patches of skin. It doesn't need to be perfect. Reserve the flesh of the fruit.

3. Julienne the Rangpur lime peel by stacking 3 or 4 pieces on top of one another and slicing them thin. Place the julienned peel in your preserving pot and set aside.

4. Now, slice the reserved fruit in half lengthwise and slice the half lengthwise again. Cut each quarter crosswise to form many small ⅛-inch-thick Rangpur lime triangles. Reserve the seeds as you go. Put the fruit slices in a medium-size nonreactive bowl as you work.

5. Once the flesh is sliced, tie up the seeds in a square of cheesecloth or scrap of white tea towel. Add them to the preserving pot with the julienned peel and cover with the water.

6. Bring to a boil, reduce heat to low, and simmer for 5 minutes. Remove from heat and pour in the sliced Rangpur lime fruit.

7. Let cool to room temperature and refrigerate overnight.

DAY TWO

1. Add the sugar and, over high heat, bring to a boil that cannot be stirred down. Cook, stirring frequently, until it passes the plate test (see page 22), about 18 minutes.

2. Ladle into prepared half-pint jars, leaving ¼-inch headspace. Remove air bubbles. Wipe rims. Place the lids on the jars and screw on the bands until they are fingertip tight.

3. Process in a water-bath canner for 10 minutes, adjusting for altitude as needed.

4. After 24 hours, check the seals. Label, date, and store out of direct sunlight without the bands for up to a year.

INGREDIENTS

1 pound rhubarb, sliced into ½-inch chunks

12 ounces (about 3 cups) raspberries

1¾ cups sugar

Yield: about 3 half pints and 1 quarter pint

MATERIALS

Basic supplies for sweet preserves (see page 18)

raspberry-RHUBARB SAUCE

A SEASONAL TOPPING FOR ICE CREAM AND CAKES WITH A QUICK COOK TIME

It takes a lot for me to pass up chocolate syrup on ice cream. I had a hot fudge sundae phase that lasted for a good chunk of my childhood, during which vanilla ice cream with hot fudge was consistently my treat of choice. However, this gorgeous, rosy-hued raspberry-rhubarb sauce is enough to get me to change my ways.

Because it's cooked just until the fruit breaks down, the final product is a versatile, spoonable sauce that's great on ice cream, over pound cake with a dollop of crème fraîche, or folded with whipped cream for a rhubarb-raspberry fool. Grab the early raspberries at the market along with the last of the rhubarb (or raid your freezer stash) for this new pantry staple.

1. In a large, nonreactive bowl, fold together the rhubarb, raspberries, and sugar. Cover and refrigerate overnight.

2. The next day, transfer the mixture to your preserving pot. Over high heat, bring the mixture to a boil that cannot be stirred down.

3. Continue cooking the sauce over high heat, stirring frequently until the rhubarb is completely broken down, likely just under 10 minutes.

4. Ladle into prepared half- and quarter-pint jars, leaving ¼-inch headspace. Remove air bubbles and wipe rims. Place the lids on the jars and screw on the bands until they are fingertip tight.

5. Process in a water-bath canner for 10 minutes, adjusting for altitude as needed.

6. After 24 hours, check the seals. Label, date, and store out of direct sunlight without the bands for up to a year.

SMOOTH CHERRY-
limeade
JAM

A REFRESHING JAM INSPIRED BY A DRIVE-IN DRINK

I didn't grow around up the fast-food drive-in, which shall remain nameless, that is known for its giant Styrofoam cups of cherry limeade. But when I first visited my mom and sister after they moved to the South, after hearing so much about this drink, it was one of the first things I tried. The tart and sweet combination totally made sense.

This cherry-limeade jam is much less sickly sweet than the fast-food version on which it's based; it combines ripe sweet cherries and both lime zest and juice to ensure plenty of pucker. Since this is a purée, and we aren't concerned with maintaining the texture of fruit pieces in a syrup, you can skip the overnight maceration step here. This cooks up incredibly fast, in less than 10 minutes. I'd begin testing around 5 to 6 minutes of cooking to ensure that you don't overcook the finished product. (It will scorch easily.)

INGREDIENTS

2 pounds (about 6 cups) pitted sweet cherries

1½ cups sugar

¼ cup fresh lime juice

2 tablespoons freshly grated lime zest

MATERIALS

Basic supplies for sweet preserves (see page 18)

Microplane or other fine grater

Immersion blender

Yield: about 3 half pints

1. Put the cherries, sugar, and lime juice in your preserving pot; stir together. Allow the mixture to sit at room temperature until about ¼ inch of juice forms on the bottom of the pot.

2. Once there's a good layer of juice in the bottom of the pot, return to high heat and bring the mixture to a boil that cannot be stirred down.

3. As soon as the mixture comes to a full rolling boil, remove from heat and carefully use an immersion blender to blend the mixture until very smooth.

4. Return the mixture to a boil over high heat, cook for 3 minutes, then add the lime zest.

5. Continue cooking the jam on high heat, stirring frequently until the mixture no longer weeps when a dollop is placed on a plate. This will happen quite quickly, likely in about 7 minutes.

6. Ladle into prepared half-pint jars, leaving ¼-inch headspace. Remove air bubbles and wipe rims. Place the lids on the jars and screw on the bands until they are fingertip tight.

7. Process in a water-bath canner for 10 minutes, adjusting for altitude as needed.

8. After 24 hours, check the seals. Label, date, and store out of direct sunlight without the bands for up to a year.

INGREDIENTS

1 pound freestone plums, such as black plums, pitted and chopped into ¼-inch chunks

14 ounces (about 3 cups) blackberries

1¾ cups sugar

1 tablespoon fresh-squeezed lemon juice

MATERIALS

Basic supplies for sweet preserves (see page 18)

Yield: about 3 half pints and 1 quarter pint

DAY ONE

1. In a large, nonreactive bowl, fold together the plums, blackberries, sugar, and lemon juice. Cover and refrigerate overnight.

DAY TWO

1. The next day, transfer the mixture to your preserving pot. Over high heat, bring the mixture to a boil that cannot be stirred down.

2. Continue cooking the jam over high heat, stirring frequently. The plums should break down and separate from their skins, and the blackberries will break down as well.

3. Cook until it passes the plate test (see page 22), about 12 minutes.

4. Ladle into prepared jars, leaving ¼-inch headspace. Remove air bubbles and wipe rims. Place the lids on the jars and screw on the bands until they are fingertip tight.

5. Process in a water-bath canner for 10 minutes, adjusting for altitude as needed.

6. After 24 hours, check the seals. Label, date, and store out of direct sunlight without the bands for up to a year.

blackberry-
PLUM JAM

ARTFULLY COMBINING FRUITS FOR A STUNNING BUT SIMPLE FLAVOR

I went through a period early in my life as a preserver during which I wanted to add additional flavor to every single jar of jam I produced. Cinnamon here, cayenne there, and cardamom pretty much everywhere. I still love playing with flavor, but I've gotten better at realizing when something might be better without my stamp on it.

It wasn't until I read *The Blue Chair Jam Cookbook* by Rachel Saunders that I truly started to appreciate the art of intentionally combining fruits and letting their simple, clean flavors shine through. This preserve is a classic example of that philosophy. Blackberries and plums are a lovely pair because their colors work together and the acidity in the plums helps balance the sweet berries. Plus, adding another fleshy fruit in with the seedy berries helps disperse the seeds in the jam and eliminates the need for straining.

STRAWBERRY PRESERVES

FEATURING TENDER ALPINE STRAWBERRIES IN A RUBY-RED SYRUP

Along with apples, strawberries are one of the fruits I make a U-pick pilgrimage for pretty much every year. And if we're being honest, I'm usually so excited for strawberries coming into season that I can't stop myself from buying some at the greenmarket before I get out to pick.

Alpine strawberries, also known as *fraise des bois*, are much smaller than commercial varieties and have a stunning, concentrated strawberry flavor. If you come across them, don't pass them by, as they're the ideal for preserving. They don't need to be hulled or cut up and produce a lovely red syrup with whole tiny fruits. In lieu of alpine strawberries, select the smallest berries available that are uniformly deep red.

INGREDIENTS

2 pounds fresh strawberries, hulled and halved, quartered, or left whole depending on the size (about 6 cups prepared)

1½ cups sugar

1 tablespoon fresh-squeezed lemon juice

MATERIALS

Basic supplies for sweet preserves (see page 18)

Yield: about 3 half pints

DAY ONE

1. Gently stir together the strawberries, sugar, and lemon juice in a large nonreactive bowl.

2. Cover and let the mixture sit at room temperature for 1 hour, then refrigerate overnight.

DAY TWO

1. Transfer the macerated fruit mixture to your preserving pot using a spatula to scrape any sugar that has settled to the bottom of the bowl.

2. Over high heat, bring the mixture to a boil that cannot be stirred down.

3. Continue to cook, stirring frequently until the mixture passes the plate test (see page 22), about 10 minutes.

4. Ladle into prepared half-pint jars, leaving ¼-inch headspace. Remove air bubbles and wipe rims. Place the lids on the jars and screw on the bands until they are fingertip tight.

5. Process in a water-bath canner for 10 minutes, adjusting for altitude as needed.

6. After 24 hours, check the seals. Label, date, and store out of direct sunlight without the bands for up to a year.

INGREDIENTS

1 half gallon apple cider or unfiltered 100 percent apple juice

Salt to taste

MATERIALS

Basic supplies for sweet preserves (see page 18)

Pint mason jar

Fine mesh strainer

NOTE: I have made this with both unpasteurized apple cider (the kind from the refrigerator section) and shelf-stable unfiltered 100 percent apple juice. Flavor-wise, either will work. The unfiltered apple juice tends to produce a more homogenous syrup. In either case, be sure to select a juice or cider that is 100 percent apples and not from concentrate.

Yield: 1 scant pint

1. Bring the cider to a boil over high heat.

2. Reduce the heat so that the cider maintains a gentle but steady simmer. Depending on your stove, about low or medium-low heat.

3. Simmer for about 1 hour and 45 minutes, or until the cider has reduced to about 1 half pint. Don't worry if it doesn't look syrupy at this point. Just like any other preserve, it will thicken as it cools.

4. Use a very fine mesh strainer or clean cotton tea towel to strain the syrup.

5. Add salt, a pinch at a time, to taste, stirring to dissolve. It should taste like your favorite salty caramel. You should be able to detect the salt flavor but not find it overwhelming.

6. Let the syrup cool to room temperature on the counter, then label and refrigerate until ready to use.

SALTED-*apple* CARAMEL

A CREATIVE TAKE ON CARAMEL THAT MAKES THE MOST OF FRESH APPLE CIDER

Boiled cider is just what it sounds like: apple cider boiled down until it reaches a syrupy consistency. The result is a sweet-tart, no-sugar-added caramel that's perfect for drizzling or using as a hot cider concentrate. I got into boiled cider one winter after adding a cider subscription to my winter CSA. I really like cider, but I'm only one woman and it began to pile up.

I love this recipe because it's infinitely flexible and totally hands-off. You can make it with a half gallon or 3 gallons, keeping in mind that the cooking time will increase as you increase the amount of cider. As an added bonus, simmering cider on your stove for hours will make your kitchen smell like all kinds of fall.

"JUST A CUP" *rosé wine* JELLY

A MICROBATCH OF JELLY WITH A SMALL AMOUNT OF LEFTOVER WINE

I'm very aware that many folks would say that there's no such thing as leftover wine. The one and only solution for what to do with leftover wine is drink it, right? Well, I'm here to argue for the unpopular opinion that leftover wine exists, and a great thing to do with it is make jelly. I can no longer count the number of times I've started a bottle of wine and forgotten about it until it was too late.

I like wine jelly and have made a number of iterations of it over the years. That said, I also like wine, and if I open a bottle I want to be able to drink some. So, I developed this microbatch wine jelly recipe. It takes just a cup of wine and makes just a half pint (or two quarter pints). That way, you can enjoy most of the bottle, save some for later, and avoid those wasted bits at the end of the bottle. And, if you can spare a cup of a bottle that you really love, I also think this is a neat way to save and remember a favorite bottle. I think rosé is especially nice for color and flavor, but any wine will work.

INGREDIENTS

¾ teaspoon Pomona's Universal Pectin powder

¼ cup plus 2 tablespoons sugar

1 cup rosé wine

½ teaspoon Pomona's Universal Pectin calcium water, prepared according to package instructions

1 tablespoon fresh-squeezed lemon juice

MATERIALS

Basic supplies for sweet preserves (see page 18)

NOTE: If you've never used Pomona's Universal Pectin, you'll find each box comes with two packets inside: one with pectin powder and one with calcium powder to make calcium water.

Yield: 2 quarter pints

1. Because recipes made with Pomona's Universal Pectin have such a short cook time, have your jars prepped and out of the water bath before you even start cooking the jelly. I like doing this in 2 quarter pints, since the batch size is so small. Because the batch is so small, you can also skip the water bath altogether and stash this in the fridge if you prefer.

2. Stir together pectin and sugar in a small bowl and set aside.

3. Combine the wine, calcium water, and lemon juice in a small saucepan. Bring to a boil over high heat.

4. As soon as the mixture comes to a boil, gradually add the pectin-sugar mixture, whisking continually to help it dissolve.

5. Cook for 1 to 2 minutes more while whisking to dissolve the pectin. Remove from the heat and use a clean spoon to skim off any foam.

6. Ladle into prepared quarter-pint jars, leaving ¼-inch headspace. Remove air bubbles and wipe rims. Place the lids on the jars and screw on the bands until they are fingertip tight.

7. Process in a water-bath canner for 10 minutes, adjusting for altitude as needed.

8. After 24 hours, check the seals. Label, date, and store out of direct sunlight without the bands for up to a year.

INGREDIENTS

2 pounds (about 5 medium) ripe yellow peaches

2 tablespoons fresh-squeezed lemon juice

1 cup sugar

2 tablespoons bourbon

MATERIALS

Basic supplies for sweet preserves (see page 18)

Yield: about 3 half pints

1. To peel the peaches: Score the bottom of each peach with a cross. Bring a pot of water large enough to hold all the peaches to a boil. Carefully lower the peaches into the boiling water and boil for 1 minute. Remove them, placing them in a colander to drain. When they're no longer too hot to touch, use your fingers to rub off the peel. Remove the pits and set the peaches aside.

2. Add the lemon juice to a large, nonreactive bowl. Roughly chop the peaches, adding them to the lemon juice and stirring as you go, to prevent browning.

3. Once all the peaches are chopped, use a potato masher to mash the fruit until you have a chunky purée. Stir in the sugar. At this point there should be enough liquid to begin cooking. If not, leave the bowl on the counter until there is.

4. Transfer the mixture to your preserving pot and bring to a boil over high heat.

5. Cook, stirring frequently, until a dollop placed on a plate no longer weeps, about 10 minutes.

6. Remove from the heat and stir in the bourbon.

7. Ladle into prepared half-pint jars, leaving ¼-inch headspace. Remove air bubbles and wipe rims. Place the lids on the jars and screw on the bands until they are fingertip tight.

8. Process in a water-bath canner for 10 minutes, adjusting for altitude as needed.

9. After 24 hours, check the seals. Label, date, and store out of direct sunlight without the bands for up to a year.

quick peach- BOURBON JAM

A QUICK JAM THAT DOESN'T COMPROMISE ON FLAVOR OR TEXTURE (AND HOW TO PREVENT FRUIT FROM BROWNING AS YOU CUT IT)

One summer, on a weekend trip to Pennsylvania, I insisted we stop at a U-pick in the area and get some peaches. When I'm at a U-pick, I mean business, so "some peaches" translates to no less than 20 pounds. I don't remember the logic behind this—it may have been geographically motivated—but we stopped at the orchard at the beginning of our trip. So the peaches sat in the hot car the rest of the weekend. Not my brightest idea ever, but the smell was amazing: honeyed, sweet, and complex.

This jam is my effort to recreate that experience, minus the poor planning. Just a bit of bourbon adds depth and caramel notes to the bright, ripe peaches. There's really no way around peeling the peaches—believe me, I checked—but, once the water is boiling, the whole process takes just a few minutes. Plus, rubbing the skins off the peaches in big swathes is oddly satisfying.

hibiscus-LIME JELLY

A POMONA'S PECTIN-BASED TEA JELLY

A beverage made from dried hibiscus flowers, known around the world as *sorrel*, *agua de Jamaica*, and a number of other names, is a tart drink rich in vitamin C and other nutrients that is sometimes compared to cranberry juice. The color is a beautiful, vibrant magenta, and the tea is served chilled in many countries as a refreshing, rehydrating beverage.

This variation on a tea jelly, of which there are many, uses the tea made from hibiscus flowers as the base for a unique, low-sugar jelly with just a touch of pucker.

INGREDIENTS

2 teaspoons Pomona's Pectin powder

½ cup sugar

2 cups boiling water

¼ cup dried hibiscus flowers

2 teaspoons calcium water (made from Pomona's Pectin calcium powder)

2 tablespoons fresh-squeezed lime juice

MATERIALS

Basic supplies for sweet preserves (see page 18)

Yield: 2 half pints

1. Because recipes made with Pomona's Pectin have such a short cook time, have your jars prepped and out of the water bath before you even start cooking the jelly.

2. Stir together the pectin and sugar in a small bowl and set aside.

3. Pour the boiling water over the hibiscus flowers in a small bowl. Let the flowers steep for 5 minutes.

4. Strain out the flowers, pressing the solids to extract as much liquid as possible.

5. Measure 2 cups of tea into a small saucepan, adding water to make up for any liquid lost in the steeping process.

6. Add the calcium water and lime juice to the saucepan. Bring to a boil over high heat.

7. As soon as the mixture comes to a boil, gradually add the pectin-sugar mixture, whisking continually to help it dissolve.

8. Cook for 1 to 2 minutes more while whisking to dissolve the pectin.

9. Remove from the heat and use a clean spoon to skim off any foam.

10. Ladle into prepared half-pint jars, leaving ¼-inch headspace. Remove air bubbles and wipe rims. Place the lids on the jars and screw on the bands until they are fingertip tight.

11. Process in a water-bath canner for 10 minutes, adjusting for altitude as needed.

12. After 24 hours, check the seals. Label, date, and store out of direct sunlight without the bands for up to a year.

banana-
CHOCOLATE
BUTTER

A certain popular chocolate-hazel-nut spread has been vilified of late for having loads of sugar and at the same time being marketed as a breakfast food. Assuming you have a food processor, it is relatively easy to make your own low- or no-sugar version of the ubiquitous spread, but all the hullabaloo got me thinking about the possibility of a fruit-based lower-sugar chocolate spread. Ba-nanas came to mind because they're naturally very sweet when ripe and they're uncannily creamy when blended. Plus, home cooks are often looking for ways to use them up!

INGREDIENTS

4 ripe bananas, peeled and broken up with your hands as you put them into the pot

1 tablespoon fresh-squeezed lemon juice

¼ cup brown sugar, lightly packed

½ teaspoon ground cinnamon

¼ cup cocoa powder

2 tablespoons maple syrup

Pinch salt

MATERIALS

Immersion blender

Yield: 1 scant pint

1. In a small stainless steel saucepan, combine all the ingredients over low heat using a wire whisk to stir and begin to break up the bananas.

2. Simmer the mixture for about 15 minutes, continuing to whisk to break up the pieces of banana as it softens.

3. Depending on the ripeness of your bananas, the whisk may be enough to create a smooth purée. Alternatively, you may remove the butter from the heat and purée with an immersion blender to make it completely smooth.

4. Transfer the butter to a pint mason jar and let cool to room temperature. Once cool, cover the jar with a two-piece lid, label, date, and refrigerate. *This recipe cannot be processed in a water-bath canner.*

INGREDIENTS

1 pound strawberries, leaves removed, but not hulled

½ cup sugar

1 tablespoon balsamic vinegar

3 sprigs fresh thyme

MATERIALS

9x9 or similar glass baking pan

Yield: 1 scant pint

1. Preheat the oven to 350°F.

2. In a large bowl, fold together the strawberries, sugar, balsamic vinegar, and thyme.

3. Turn the mixture onto the baking sheet, spreading it into an even layer.

4. Bake at 350°F for 35 minutes, stirring twice in the first 20 minutes.

5. Let cool to room temperature and transfer to a container using a spatula to scrape all the juices that will collect during roasting. Label, date, and refrigerate until ready to use.

RESCUE-ROASTED *strawberry* COMPOTE WITH THYME

A SIMPLE WAY TO EXTEND THE LIFE OF STRAWBERRIES THAT ARE PAST THEIR PRIME

The reality of preserving is that it happens in the real world—in messy kitchens, during crazy workweeks, in houses with unexpected visitors. And while it would be lovely to pick strawberries and preserve them the same day, I have never been so lucky. This recipe is a nod to the fact that sometimes preserving is just the quickest, easiest way of keeping something from spoiling. Roasting can also vastly improve early or out-of-season strawberries whose quality ends up being a letdown.

Cooking down strawberries via roasting transforms them into a surprisingly jammy compote with much less effort than it takes to make a traditional preserve. Jar and refrigerate the compote with the spent thyme sprigs to infuse additional thyme flavor and then use it any way you'd use jam—in your morning oatmeal, spooned over ice cream, or swirled into yogurt.

RUSTIC
jumbleberry-
PIE JAM

FEATURING ALL THE SUMMER BERRIES AND A HIT OF VANILLA

My mom, who is not really a sweet-treat fanatic like I am, loves jumble-berry pie. Each year for her birthday, and pretty much every holiday, we'd pick up a fresh jumbleberry pie at a little restaurant in my hometown. It was what she always asked for. Jumbleberry is just what it sounds like: a jumble of summer berries. Here it's strawberries, blackberries, and blueberries.

As a purist I can confidently assert that this isn't a jam for purists. This one is pure nostalgia. There are all sorts of arguments against a preserve like this: you lose the color of the strawberries because they're stained a deep blackberry purple, the flavors of each berry get somewhat lost in the others, the blackberries break down much more than the others, and so on. However, the argument *for* it is the only one that matters: it's really, really delicious. More than any other recipe in this book, this one tastes like summer.

INGREDIENTS

1 vanilla bean

12 ounces strawberries (about 2¼ cups), chopped into approximately ¼-inch chunks

12 ounces (about 2¾ cups) blackberries

12 ounces (about 2½ cups) blueberries

2 cups sugar

Zest and juice of 1 lemon

MATERIALS

Basic supplies for sweet preserves (see page 18)

Microplane or other fine grater

Potato masher

Yield: 2 quarter pints

To prepare the jam:

1. Using a sharp knife, split the vanilla bean lengthwise and scrape out the seeds.

2. In a large, nonreactive bowl, stir together the berries, vanilla bean seeds and pod, sugar, and lemon juice and zest. Mash the mixture with a potato masher to begin breaking down the berries.

3. Let the mixture macerate at room temperature for 1 hour or up to overnight.

4. Transfer the macerated fruit mixture to your preserving pot using a spatula to scrape any sugar that has settled to the bottom of the bowl.

5. Over high heat, bring the mixture to a boil that cannot be stirred down.

6. Cook, stirring frequently, until the mixture passes the plate test (see page 22), about 7 minutes. Remove the vanilla bean pod and discard.

7. Ladle into prepared half-pint jars, leaving ¼-inch headspace. Remove air bubbles and wipe rims. Place the lids on the jars and screw on the bands until they are fingertip tight.

8. Process in a water-bath canner for 10 minutes, adjusting for altitude as needed.

9. After 24 hours, check the seals. Label, date, and store out of direct sunlight without the bands for up to a year.

INGREDIENTS

1 teaspoon fennel seeds

1 pound fresh green figs, cut into ½-inch chunks

1 cup sugar

2 tablespoons bottled lemon juice

½ teaspoon balsamic vinegar

MATERIALS

Basic supplies for sweet preserves (see page 18)

Small stainless steel skillet

Mortar and pestle or spice grinder

FIG JAM
WITH TOASTED
fennel seeds

Yield: 2 half pints

1. To toast the fennel seeds, heat them in a bare stainless steel skillet until they're aromatic and just start to darken. This won't take more than a couple of minutes. Use a mortar and pestle or spice grinder to grind them into a coarse powder.

2. In a large nonreactive bowl, fold together the figs, sugar, and lemon juice. Add the fennel seeds and let the mixture macerate for at least 4 hours or up to overnight.

3. Transfer the mixture to your preserving pot using a spatula to scrape any sugar that has settled to the bottom of the bowl and, over high heat, bring to a boil that can't be stirred down.

4. Cook until the mixture passes the plate test (see page 22), about 7 minutes. Remove from the heat and stir in the balsamic vinegar.

5. Ladle into prepared quarter-pint jars, leaving ¼-inch headspace. Remove air bubbles and wipe rims. Place the lids on the jars and screw on the bands until they are fingertip tight.

6. Process in a water-bath canner for 15 minutes, adjusting for altitude as needed.

7. After 24 hours, check the seals. Label, date, and store out of direct sunlight without the bands for up to a year.

A SWEET PRESERVE WITH A SAVORY CHARACTER

Before living in the desert, I considered figs a rarity—a somewhat mythical, hard-to-transport fruit that was often out of my price range. When I lived in Queens, there was a fig tree in a nearby yard that I would visit just to admire and check on its progress.

And just so the next statement doesn't seem like I'm bragging *too* much, there are plenty of things that don't grow well in the desert. As you might guess, there aren't any U-pick berry operations in my neck of the woods. That said, we can grow figs, and we can grow them darn well. When monsoon season starts at the beginning of July, the fig trees explode. It's truly magical.

Even with the added lemon juice, which provides the necessary acid to can the figs safely, the figs are quite sweet. Just a touch of balsamic vinegar added at the end of the cooking period adds balance and brings out the savory side of the figs and fennel.

orange- ROSEWATER CURD

FEATURING A SECRET HIT OF LEMON JUICE FOR THE PERFECT POP

Every year during citrus season, I make at least one batch of curd. I tend to cycle through favorite recipes. For a while I was using David Lebovitz's Improved Meyer Lemon Curd recipe, which is either quite stressful or quite great—depending on your opinion—because it doesn't call for a double boiler. The past couple of years, I've been devoted to the lime curd recipe from Kevin West's *Saving the Season*, which is fantastic.

Oranges can be a bit unwieldy in a curd. Orange curd risks falling a bit flat flavorwise because oranges are less acidic than lemons and limes. To address that here, we're punching up the acidity of the orange juice with a little lemon juice. It's not enough to make it taste like lemons, but it does add a bit of necessary pucker. Finally, we're adding just a hint of floral aroma with a dash of rosewater at the end. If you're one of those folks who thinks rosewater tastes like soap, you can omit the rosewater and/or swap in another complementary flavor that you prefer, such as vanilla.

INGREDIENTS

Zest of 2 oranges

½ cup fresh-squeezed orange juice (2 to 3 oranges)

2 tablespoons fresh-squeezed lemon juice

½ cup sugar

6 egg yolks

1 stick (8 tablespoons) butter, cut into 8 pieces

¼ teaspoon rosewater, or more to taste

MATERIALS

Fine mesh strainer

Microplane or other fine grater

Probe thermometer (optional)

Yield: 1 scant pint

1. Position a fine mesh strainer over a medium-size nonreactive bowl.

2. Combine the orange zest, orange juice, lemon juice, sugar, and egg yolks in a double boiler. If you're like me, you can make a makeshift one by positioning a stainless steel bowl over a small saucepan containing a couple inches of water.

3. Whisk to combine the mixture completely.

4. Cook over low heat, gradually adding the butter 1 piece at a time and letting it melt completely before adding more. This will happen slowly at first and more rapidly as the curd heats up. Whisk constantly during this process.

5. After all the butter has been added, continue cooking until the mixture reaches 170°F. A thermometer is useful here because it allows you to cook the curd to the point of just being done, but not overdone. Alternatively, it should coat the back of a spoon like a pudding or custard.

6. Immediately remove the curd from the heat and pour it through the fine mesh strainer. This will remove the pieces of zest and any tiny bits of egg that got cooked. You can gently stir the mixture to help it pass through the sieve, but do not crush. Stir the rosewater into the strained curd.

7. Transfer the curd to a pint mason jar and let cool to room temperature. Once cool, cover the jar with a 2-piece lid, label, and refrigerate. *The curd cannot be processed in a water-bath canner.*

INGREDIENTS

1 tablespoon fresh-squeezed lemon juice

3 pounds (about 5 medium) ripe but firm Bartlett pears, cored, peeled, and cut into ½-inch chunks

½ cup sugar

1 teaspoon ground cardamom

MATERIALS

Basic supplies for sweet preserves (see page 18)

Immersion blender

Yield: 2 half pints

1. Place the lemon juice in your preserving pot. Add the first 2 pears and mash them with a potato masher to create the liquid to help the mixture begin cooking. Add the remaining pears and begin cooking over low heat.

2. As the fruit begins to cook and release its liquid, you can increase the heat to medium-low and use your spatula to help break apart the pieces of pear.

3. Cook until the pears are easily smooshed with the back of a spatula.

4. Remove from the heat and carefully use an immersion blender to blend the mixture into a very smooth purée, like the consistency of baby food. It sounds unappetizing now, but it will make your final product velvety.

5. Return the pear purée to your preserving pot, add the sugar and cardamom, and return to medium-low heat. Stir more frequently at the end of the cooking time, and reduce the heat to low if necessary to prevent scorching. The mixture will sputter quite a bit, but you don't want to cover it. I'll usually set a lid just partially on to help control the hot spatters of pear purée, but still allow the mixture to evaporate.

6. Cook until a dollop on a plate mounds and does not weep juice around the edges, about 1 hour and 15 minutes.

RECIPE CONTINUES ON PAGE 72

PEAR- *cardamom* BUTTER

A SPICED FRUIT BUTTER WHERE OPPOSITE INTENSITIES ATTRACT

Pears and cardamom are a slightly odd couple. Pears have quite a subtle flavor, and cardamom is rather bold. In theory, cardamom should overwhelm the pear, but in reality the result is something quite different—it provides a lovely contrast. Because I'm obsessed with cardamom, I limited myself to including it in one sweet preserve recipe in the book, and this was the winner.

Although this recipe starts with more fruit than most others in the book—3 pounds—the amount of cooking down that goes into pear butter still makes this a small-batch preserve, with a yield of just 2 half pints. Rather than leaving on the peel and using a food mill, as in the apple butter recipe, I like to prep the pears for this by peeling and coring them—a tip I learned from the preserving writer and educator Sheri Brooks Vinton. This can help eliminate the portions of the pear that give it a somewhat grainy texture. It's a little more meticulous, but definitely worth it.

PREPPING PEARS TO AVOID GRAININESS

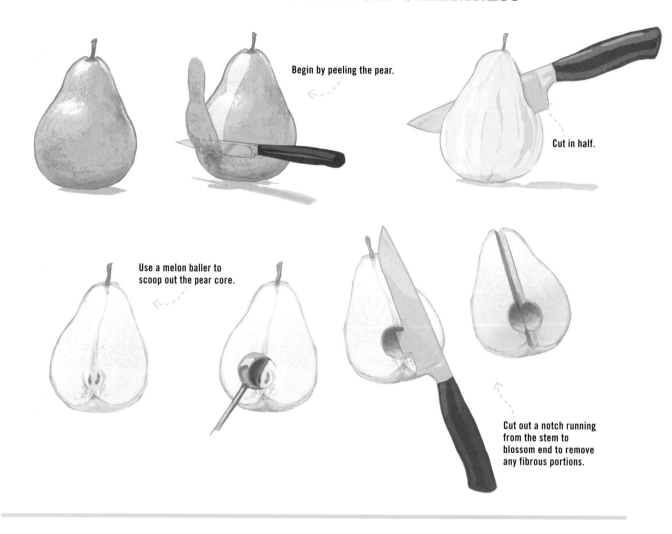

Begin by peeling the pear.

Cut in half.

Use a melon baller to scoop out the pear core.

Cut out a notch running from the stem to blossom end to remove any fibrous portions.

7. Ladle into prepared half-pint jars, leaving ¼-inch headspace. Remove air bubbles and wipe rims. Place the lids on the jars and screw on the bands until they are fingertip tight.

8. Process in a water-bath canner for 10 minutes, adjusting for altitude as needed.

9. After 24 hours, check the seals. Label, date, and store out of direct sunlight without the bands for up to a year.

INGREDIENTS

1¼ cups old-fashioned oats

1 cup almond flour

½ cup oat flour

½ cup buckwheat flour

½ cup light brown sugar, lightly packed

½ teaspoon salt

1½ sticks unsalted butter, heated just until it is melted

1 egg yolk

½ pint sweet preserve of your choice

MATERIALS

8x8 baking dish lined with parchment paper

Yield: one 8x8 baking dish, 9 to 12 servings depending on how small you cut them

1. Preheat the oven to 350°F.

2. Whisk together the oats, almond flour, oat flour, buckwheat flour, brown sugar, and salt, breaking up any clumps using your spatula.

3. Make a well in the center and pour in the butter and egg yolk. Stir vigorously to fully incorporate the egg and butter.

4. Press a little more than half the dough into the parchment-lined baking dish. The back of a spoon works especially well for this.

5. Gently spread the jam evenly on top of the bottom layer of dough.

6. Crumble the rest of the dough over the jam layer.

7. Bake for 30 to 35 minutes or until it begins to brown. Cool, use the edges of the parchment to lift the bars out of the pan, and cut the bars into squares.

buckwheat-OAT JAM CRUMB BARS

A WHOLE-GRAIN BAR COOKIE THAT'S TOTALLY ACCEPTABLE FOR BREAKFAST

I really can't get enough of pairing sweet preserves with whole grains. It isn't a coincidence that folks have been stirring jam into their oatmeal for years and years. The hearty, nutty taste of whole grains is a perfect foil for sweet, fruity preserves.

This recipe is a mash-up of two of my favorite baked treats that feature sweet preserves: a buckwheat flour thumbprint cookie and an oat-studded jam crumb bar featuring almond flour. What I love about this recipe is that there's just one dough. You mix it up, use some for the crust, layer on the preserves, and crumble the rest of the dough on top. In other words, this is a one-bowl affair. An egg yolk helps act as a binder for these whole-grain flours that have less elasticity. The jam flavor is up to you!

PICKLING

I AM A FIRM BELIEVER IN THE POWER OF condiments. I am absolutely confident that a pickle, relish, chutney, or ketchup can make or break a meal. Particularly those humble meals like a slice of bread and cheese, grains and beans, eggs, roasted winter roots, or the almighty leftover. The recipes in this chapter use the technique of vinegar pickling to preserve, certainly, but also to ensure that you always have something on hand to elevate a simple meal to something special.

Just as the previous chapter on sweet preserves doesn't have that many jam recipes, strictly speaking, I must confess that this pickle chapter doesn't have that many traditional pickle recipes. There's not a cucumber in a jar in the whole lot! What you'll find instead are plenty of new takes on vegetables and fruits pickled using water-bath canning, like the Pickled Mandarinquats with Ginger & Pink Peppercorns on page 90. You'll also find fridge pickles using a variety of vinegars, and refreshing drinking vinegars called shrubs. As in all the recipes in this book, the batches are small, so you can find something that you love without making a big investment.

There are definitely a few darn fine jars of pickles to follow, like the Smoky Carrot Coins on page 116, that are great straight out of the jar. However, in my experience, vinegar-based preserves are at their best and most practical as quick tools to add flavor, texture, and pucker to the stuff you're already eating.

THE FRUITS & VEGETABLES

The recipes that follow employ fruits and vegetables in nearly equal measure. In my ideal world, we'd all have access to and be able to afford unsprayed and/or organic produce. So, at the risk of sounding like a broken record, I'll tell you again that when it's possible, organic, low-spray, unsprayed, or backyard fruit or vegetables are best. That said, many of the vegetable pickles in this book involve peeling, so selecting organic produce for those recipes is somewhat less important. Conversely, for the citrus pickles that use peel and all, like the marmalades in the previous chapter, selecting organic, low-spray, unsprayed, or backyard fruit is more of a priority. Just as with sweet preserves, choose the best-quality produce you can.

THE SALT

Perhaps you've heard of or seen pickling salt in the canning aisle of your grocery or hardware store. Salt marketed as pickling salt is sodium chloride, just like standard table salt, but has no anticaking agents or iodine. It is made to dissolve quickly, so it is quite fine grain. I've sought out pickling salt in the past but only found it available in very large quantities and—because it has no anticaking agents—it turned to a solid block before I could use it up. Using a salt that does contain iodine and/or an anticaking agent won't compromise the safety of your pickle, but it may have aesthetic consequences such as a slightly cloudy brine or white flakes. I recommend what I think is a more practical solution, which is seeking out a kosher salt or sea salt without an anticaking agent, which you can use for your regular cooking and baking as well as the ferments in the next chapter; if you use it often, it won't have an opportunity to cake up. All of the recipes in this chapter were developed using a kosher salt without an anticaking agent.

THE VINEGAR

The type of vinegar you use for each of the following recipes is very important; each one has been selected with both taste and safety in mind. All vinegars are not created equal.

For the recipes in this chapter that use water-bath canning as a method of preservation, you must use distilled white or apple cider vinegar (not raw) that has been diluted to 5 percent acidity. Check the label to confirm that the vinegar is 5 percent acidity, and if you can't find that information on the label, don't use it. In general, distilled white vinegar has a slightly sharper but more neutral taste than apple cider vinegar, which is less sharp and more fruity. Other types of vinegars cannot be substituted in the recipes where a 5 percent acidity vinegar is required.

Fridge pickles are a different story. The recipes that follow for vinegar-based preserves that are not processed in a water-bath canner use a variety of vinegars. These preserves don't need the standardized acidity of 5 percent for safety, unless noted, so a wider variety of vinegars can be used, depending on the desired taste and flavor.

Rice vinegar is clean and mild, making it perfect for recipes like the Kombu Dashi Pickled Shiitake Mushrooms on page 82. White wine and red wine vinegar are fairly neutral, although slightly sweet, with a bit more acidity than something like rice vinegar, making them great for the drinking vinegars called shrubs. Select white wine vinegar or red wine vinegar to complement the color of the finished product— white for lighter-colored foods, red for berries and other darker foods. Balsamic vinegar imparts caramelized notes and, of course, a brown color unless you seek out white balsamic vinegar. Keeping the differences in flavor and color in mind, when you're experimenting with vinegar-based preserves that aren't processed in a water-bath canner, you have more flexibility around which vinegar you choose.

THE STUFF

For the vinegar-based preserves in this chapter that are processed in a water-bath canner, the equipment is the same as that described for processing sweet preserves in the last chapter (page 18). The nice-to-have items for sweet preserves are nice to have for vinegar-based preserves as well.

BASIC SUPPLIES FOR VINEGAR PRESERVES

You'll want to round up the following basic equipment before you get started putting your pickles in jars:

- Mason jars with two-piece lid closure; you'll mostly use pint and half-pint jars in this chapter
- Jar lifter
- Tall stockpot with a lid and silicone trivet for processing
- Wooden chopstick
- Wide-mouth canning funnel
- Clean kitchen towel
- Paper towels
- Spatula
- Heavy-bottom preserving pot
- Ladle
- Large nonreactive bowl

THE PROCESS

For the vinegar-based preserves in this chapter that are processed in a water-bath canner, the process is the same as that described for processing sweet preserves in the last chapter on page 20. Note, however, that most of the recipes that following in this chapter ask that you allow for ½-inch headspace, rather than ¼ inch, as with sweet preserves. For those that aren't processed in a water-bath canner, the techniques will vary from recipe to recipe.

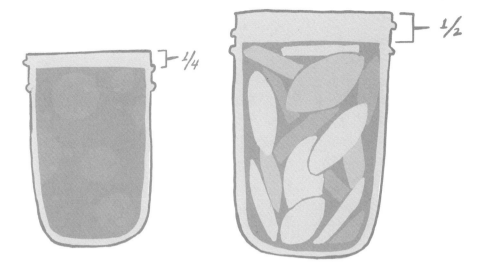

NOW WE WAIT

Although it is safe to immediately consume vinegar-based preserves that have been water-bath canned and those that haven't, it is best to wait. For a recipe like the Rhubarb-Cardamom Chutney on page 80, which is processed in a water bath, I recommend waiting two weeks before popping open the jars. I use two weeks as a general rule for how long a water-bath canned, vinegar-based preserve should cure to develop optimum flavor. For vinegar-based preserves that that have a shorter shelf life and just get a stay in the fridge, you don't need to wait two weeks, but know that their flavors will mellow and meld the longer they sit.

THE CASE FOR NOT CANNING . . . SOMETIMES

When I first started canning, I made a tomatillo sauce, basically a slightly runnier tomatillo salsa, that was intended as a simmer sauce for meat or vegetables. This recipe was the first thing I canned on my own, so I was not only a little on edge but double-checked every aspect of the ingredients and directions. Everything went well, until I opened the sauce—it tasted more like lemons than tomatillos and peppers. Well, I realized it was because the sauce required such a large amount of bottled lemon juice to be water-bath canned safely, that it was really no surprise it tasted like lemons. From then on, I made the tomatillo sauce how I liked it, and froze it rather than canning it.

By the same token, there are recipes, like the Banana Ketchup on page 105, that I think would suffer if made safe for water-bath canning. Bananas are a low-acid fruit, below the safe threshold for water-bath canning without acidification. However, significantly acidifying this recipe impacts the taste negatively. Does this mean that the banana ketchup takes up space in the fridge? Yes. Does it mean you'll make smaller batches more often? Also yes, but it's going to taste better.

rhubarb-CARDAMOM CHUTNEY

CARDAMOM AND TART RHUBARB TOGETHER IN A CHUTNEY THAT WILL BE THE STAR OF YOUR CHEESE PLATE

Cardamom is my all-time favorite spice. Although I enjoy it in combination with many things, the recipes in the book where I decided to include it were the places I knew it would truly shine, like this rhubarb chutney. It provides the perfect contrast for the tart, vegetal rhubarb.

Whenever I preserve rhubarb, I always have the color in mind. The vibrant pink stalks are such a welcome sight in greenmarkets in the spring that it seems like such a shame when that color often largely fades after cooking. I'm all for ugly, delicious food, but I live in a pink house. I'm partial to the color pink. To remedy this and help keep my rhubarb from appearing too murky, I often try to pair it with like-colored ingredients that are also compatible in terms of flavor. In this case, dried cherries instead of raisins and white sugar instead of brown. The result is a chutney with a concentrated rhubarb flavor and plenty of spicy complexity. It's a cheese plate game changer and goes especially well with roast pork and pork chops.

INGREDIENTS

¾ cup granulated sugar

½ teaspoon kosher salt

1 tablespoon ground cardamom

2 tablespoons whole yellow mustard seed

⅓ cup diced white onion

½ cup dried cherries, coarsely chopped

1 tablespoon grated fresh ginger

1 pound rhubarb, trimmed and sliced into ½-inch chunks

¾ cup apple cider vinegar

MATERIALS

Basic supplies for vinegar preserves (see page 78)

Yield: about 2 half pints

1. Combine all of the ingredients in your preserving pot.

2. Over high heat, bring the mixture to a boil that cannot be stirred down. Stir frequently as it comes to a boil.

3. Reduce the heat to low and simmer until the mixture has thickened and the rhubarb has broken down completely, about 20 minutes. Toward the end of the cooking time it may be necessary to stir the chutney more frequently to prevent scorching.

4. Ladle into prepared half-pint jars, leaving ½-inch headspace. Remove air bubbles and wipe rims. Place the lids on the jars and screw on the bands until they're fingertip tight.

5. Process in a water-bath canner for 10 minutes, adjusting for altitude if needed.

6. After 24 hours, check the seals. Label, date, and store out of direct sunlight without the bands for up to a year.

kombu dashi PICKLED SHIITAKE MUSHROOMS

FEATURING A SEAWEED-INFUSED, BROTH-INSPIRED BRINE

Kombu dashi, a simple stock made of seaweed and water, is essential to Japanese cooking. Traditionally, dried fish is added to the stock, but vegetarian versions often include shiitake mushrooms in its place. Taking the flavors of kombu dashi broth as inspiration, this fridge pickle uses mild rice vinegar, kombu, and tamari as a brine for fresh shiitake mushrooms. The result is a pickle that, like kombu dashi, combines simple, clean flavors for a ton of umami.

These are absolutely the perfect add-in to have on hand for fried rice. I have a bit of a reputation for what has come to be known as an "Autumn Scramble," which is basically all the odds and ends and leftovers in the fridge, sautéed together, sometimes with an egg scrambled in. This chewy, puckery pickle often makes its way into Autumn Scrambles and is great for dressing up other leftovers as well.

INGREDIENTS

2 cups water

1 4-inch-square piece of kombu

½ cup rice vinegar

2 tablespoons thinly sliced scallions

2 teaspoons tamari or soy sauce

1 tablespoon sugar

4 ounces fresh shiitake mushrooms, stems removed (see sidebar), wiped clean with a damp paper towel, left whole if small enough or cut into bite-size pieces

MATERIALS

Basic supplies for vinegar preserves (see page 78)

Yield: about 1 pint

1. Combine the water, kombu, rice vinegar, scallions, soy sauce, and sugar in your preserving pot and begin to bring to a boil over high heat.

2. Stir to dissolve the sugar (it should take just 1 or 2 minutes), then add the mushrooms.

3. When mixture boils, reduce the heat to low and simmer for 20 minutes. The mushrooms should be tender.

4. Let the mixture cool to room temperature, then remove the kombu. If small pieces have broken off, don't worry about them. Just remove the large sheet.

5. Cover, label, and store the pickles in a pint jar in the fridge. *These pickles cannot be safely processed in a water-bath canner.*

SAVE THE STEMS

I was once reprimanded by a complete stranger in the packed Union Square Greenmarket in New York City for breaking the stem off a portobello mushroom before buying it. According to her, I was doing an injustice to the best part of the mushroom. I begged to differ about the often-woody portobello stem. I'm cheap, I had no shame, and the thing was huge. I wasn't about to pay for it just to throw it away at home. (I now know it's possible to use these things for stock.) Weirder things happened to me in my time living in New York, but this one stuck with me because I always wondered if

she was privy to some portobello secrets that I wasn't.

Fast forward a few years and I read *The Gift of Healing Herbs*, a fabulous, accessible book on herbal medicine by Robin Rose Bennett. In it she recommends saving shiitake stems and infusing them in vinegar for a delicious vinegar with all the good properties of shiitake mushrooms. You can probably guess who this made me think of! I suggest you do the same when you make a batch of these pickled shiitakes. Cover the stems with apple cider vinegar and let steep at room temperature for at least a week or up to two.

broiled PICKLED ONIONS

AN EASY WAY TO ADD RICH ONION FLAVOR TO ANY DISH

As a long-time city and apartment dweller, I've never owned a grill. It hasn't been in the cards for me, no matter how badly I wanted one—and I wanted one *bad*. The positive side to being grill-less for all of my adult life thus far is that I've had plenty of time to explore the many ways of imparting smoky flavor without a grill. Chipotle powder and smoked paprika are favorites of mine, as you may have noticed, as is the trusty broiler.

It's hard to improve on a classic like pickled onions, but giving them a quick run under the broiler before pickling both softens them slightly and gives them an awesome charred flavor. In general, pickled onions are nice because they mean you have onions prepped, cut, and ready to go come dinnertime. I find I'm much more likely to use them when that's the case.

INGREDIENTS

1 pound 2 ounces white onions (about 2 medium), cut into rings

2 cups distilled white vinegar

1 cup water

¼ teaspoon salt

¼ cup sugar

FOR EACH JAR:

¼ teaspoon whole yellow mustard seed

¼ teaspoon celery seed

MATERIALS

Basic supplies for vinegar preserves (see page 78)

Rimmed, foil-lined baking sheet

Yield: 2 pints

1. Lay the onions in a single layer on the foil-lined baking sheet.

2. Stick them under the broiler until about half are just beginning to blacken on the edges. Broilers can vary so much that it's best to just keep an eye on them.

3. Once the onions have blackened, combine the vinegar, water, salt, and sugar in a medium saucepan.

4. Over high heat, stir the mixture to dissolve the salt and sugar. Once the salt and sugar are dissolved, add the onions and bring everything to a boil.

5. As soon as the brine comes to a boil, reduce the heat to low and simmer for 5 minutes. Remove from heat.

6. Place the mustard seeds and celery seeds in each prepared jar.

7. Ladle the onion into the prepared pint jars, evenly distributing them and then the brine, leaving ½-inch headspace. Remove air bubbles and wipe rims. Place the lids on the jars and screw on the bands until they are fingertip tight.

8. Process in a water-bath canner for 10 minutes, adjusting for altitude if needed.

9. After 24 hours, check the seals. Label, date, and store out of direct sunlight without the bands for up to a year.

blackberry-SAGE SHRUB

INGREDIENTS

FOR THE BLACKBERRY SHRUB SYRUP:

2 cups fresh blackberries

1¼ cups sugar

FOR THE SAGE-INFUSED VINEGAR:

¼ cup roughly chopped fresh sage

½ cup raw apple cider vinegar

MATERIALS

Quart mason jar

Pint mason jar

Fine mesh strainer

Medium nonreactive bowl

Yield: 1 scant pint

A FLAVORED SHRUB WITH INFUSED VINEGAR

Shrubs are a quick, easy way to preserve a small (or large, if you want to scale up) quantity of fragile, fresh berries. Fruity, tart vinegar syrups, shrubs are also called "drinking vinegars," as they're made to be added to soda water or cocktails. Just like many of the preserves in this book, shrubs start with a maceration period. Although you can make shrubs using a cooked syrup, the benefit of cold-process shrubs is both ease and the bright, clean flavor of raw berries in the finished product.

Because the degree to which herbs impart their flavor during the maceration process is inconsistent at best, a more reliable method is to infuse the vinegar with herbs at the same time that the berries are macerating. In my experience, this is a more effective way of getting the flavor of fresh herbs into a shrub syrup. Although the 3-day maceration period is time enough to produce a good infused vinegar, if you think to jumpstart it by a week or so, the flavor will be even more pronounced.

1. In a quart mason jar combine the blackberries and sugar. Use a wooden spoon or its handle—whichever fits—to smash the blackberries right in the jar. You don't need a mush, but there should be no whole blackberries left.

2. Cover the jar with a two-piece mason jar lid and shake to evenly distribute the sugar.

3. Let the blackberries and sugar sit at room temperature for 1 hour, then transfer to the refrigerator for 3 days.

4. At the same time that you combine the blackberries and sugar, place the fresh sage in a pint mason jar, then cover it with the raw apple cider vinegar. The vinegar and herbs can infuse at room temperature.

5. After 3 days, pour the sage and vinegar mixture (don't worry, we'll strain it later) into the jar with the blackberries and sugar.

Smash the berries only until there are no whole ones left.

6. Shake the vinegar with the blackberries and sugar to dissolve any remaining sugar.

7. Once all the sugar is dissolved, position a fine mesh strainer over a medium bowl.

8. Strain the syrup, gently pressing the blackberry solids to extract as much liquid as possible without forcing solids through the sieve.

9. Cover, label, and refrigerate the strained syrup in a pint mason jar until ready to use.

INGREDIENTS

2 cups trimmed and sliced celery, ¼ inch thick

1 cup sugar

½ teaspoon coarsely ground black pepper

½ cup white wine vinegar

MATERIALS

Quart mason jar

Pint mason jar

Fine mesh strainer

Medium nonreactive bowl

Yield: 1 scant pint

1. In a quart mason jar, combine the celery, sugar, and pepper. Use a wooden spoon or its handle—whichever fits best—to bruise the celery slightly.

2. Cover the jar with a two-piece mason jar lid and shake to evenly distribute the sugar.

3. Let the mixture sit at room temperature for 1 hour then transfer to the refrigerator for 3 days.

4. After 3 days, pour the vinegar into the jar with the celery, sugar, and black pepper. Shake to dissolve any remaining sugar. Once all the sugar is dissolved, position a fine mesh strainer over a medium bowl.

5. Strain the syrup, pressing the celery solids to extract as much liquid as possible without forcing solids through the sieve.

6. Cover, label, and refrigerate the strained syrup in a pint mason jar until ready to use.

CELERY & *black pepper* SHRUB

A SAVORY TAKE ON SHRUB SYRUP

I became a bit obsessed with the herb lovage when I first discovered it. It looks and tastes a lot like celery leaves but a bit more mild and without the bitterness. In my experiments with it, I made a simple syrup infused with lovage, drank celery-flavored sodas all summer, and never looked back. I don't particularly like to eat celery, but I could drink it all day. It's a super-refreshing flavor, but the first sip of celery soda definitely involves a little leap of faith. The problem with lovage, unless you grow it yourself, is it can be a bit hard to track down.

Celery, on the other hand, is everywhere. While not one of the usual suspects, celery makes so much sense for a cold-process shrub. Because of its high water content, it releases a ton of juice in the maceration process, just like berries, imparting a true celery flavor without the need for juicing or infusing. Another of my surprise favorite syrup ingredients, the humble black peppercorn, infuses the syrup with a mild spice that is a perfect companion to the cool celery. Serve with seltzer and, if you're a gin lover like me, a splash of gin.

PICKLED
MANDARINQUATS
with ginger & pink
PEPPERCORNS

INGREDIENTS

8 ounces mandarinquats (about 10), halved

1 cup distilled white vinegar

½ cup sugar

¼ teaspoon ground ginger

¼ teaspoon whole pink peppercorns

Pinch salt

MATERIALS

Basic supplies for vinegar preserves (see page 78)

Yield: about 2 half pints

A PIQUANT, WHOLE-CITRUS PICKLE

As much as I love the utility and tradition of spending a sweaty late-summer weekend turning a box of tomatoes into sauce, for me, canning is just as often about making something that feels worthy out of a rare, special thing. A couple of handfuls of mandarinquats are a perfect example of this. A mandarinquat is just what it sounds like, a cross between a mandarin orange and a kumquat. Like kumquats, mandarinquats have a relatively thin, edible skin, making them an ideal candidate for a whole-citrus pickle.

My love for salt-pickled lemons (AKA preserved lemons) knows no bounds, so when my friend Kate of the *Hip Girl's Guide to Homemaking* passed along a vinegar-pickled citrus recipe, my interest was definitely piqued. Like salt-preserved citrus, this is a skin-and-all situation. Although simmered to soften first, the skin retains its chew. Best of all, once you open the jar, the pickling liquid doubles as a citrusy shrub.

1. In your preserving pot, cover the mandarinquats with cold water by 1 inch and bring to boil that cannot be stirred down.

2. Immediately reduce heat to low and simmer until the mandarinquats can easily be pierced with a wooden chopstick, about 30 minutes. Add more water if needed.

3. Drain the mandarinquats, discarding their cooking liquid. Set aside in a separate bowl.

4. Combine the vinegar, sugar, ground ginger, pink peppercorns, and salt in your preserving pot and begin to bring to a boil over high heat. (You can use the same one that you just simmered the fruit in.)

5. Stir to dissolve the sugar and salt. Once they're dissolved, add the fruit and bring to a boil. Lower the heat and simmer for 5 minutes.

6. Ladle the mandarinquats into the prepared half-pint jars, evenly distributing them between the 2 jars and leaving ½-inch headspace. Remove air bubbles and wipe rims. Place the lids on the jars and screw on the bands until they are fingertip tight.

7. Process in a water-bath canner for 10 minutes, adjusting for altitude if needed.

8. After 24 hours, check the seals. Label, date, and store out of direct sunlight without the bands for up to a year.

INGREDIENTS

1½ pounds Valencia oranges (about 3 large)

1 cup apple cider vinegar

1 cup sugar

1½ teaspoons curry powder

Pinch salt

MATERIALS

Basic supplies for vinegar preserves (see page 78)

Food processor

Yield: about 2 half pints and 1 quarter pint

1. Cut the peel off the oranges in 1-inch strips, leaving behind as much pith as possible.

2. Cover the peels with water by 2 inches and bring to a boil over high heat. Reduce heat and simmer the peels for 1 hour.

3. In the meantime, remove any remaining white pith from the oranges.

4. Slice the oranges in half along their equators, popping out any visible seeds. Cut each half into 4 sections and set aside, continuing to remove the seeds as you work.

5. After 1 hour, carefully strain the peels and discard the cooking water.

6. Add the strips of tender peel and the chunks of fresh orange to a food processor and pulse until you have a rough purée, like a rough-cut marmalade.

7. Transfer the mixture to your preserving pot and add the vinegar, sugar, curry powder, and pinch of salt.

8. Bring to a boil, then reduce heat and simmer the mixture for 20 minutes, or until it thickens slightly.

9. Ladle the pickle into the prepared half- and quarter-pint jars, leaving ½-inch headspace. Remove air bubbles and wipe rims. Place the lids on the jars and screw on the bands until they are fingertip tight.

10. Process in a water-bath canner for 10 minutes, adjusting for altitude if needed.

11. After 24 hours, check the seals. Label, date, and store out of direct sunlight without the bands for up to a year.

CURRIED ORANGE PICKLE

A SAVORY, CITRUSY RELISH

This recipe was one of my white whales—I tested it more than any other in the book, hands down. I cut and reintroduced it into the book a few times, but now that I have it working like a charm, perhaps not surprisingly, it's one of my favorites.

When I first started thinking about this recipe, I was calling it an "orange pickle," after the Indian salt-preserved citrus condiment. Because, like a lime pickle, it's a citrus pickle dressed up with spice, it was an orange pickle in my notes for a long time. As it evolved, it became a relish for a while and a chutney for a bit, but it ended up back where it started as a pickle because it shares that put-it-on-everything quality with Indian lime pickle.

My friend Shae, who writes the preserving site Hitchhiking to Heaven, has this genius method for making a marmalade-jam hybrid using whole citrus—skin, juice, membranes, and all. Because her hack both involves skin and all and simplifies a some-times-multistep process, I love it! I'm appropriating it here for a vinegary citrus relish that is sweet and puckery like a chutney, with the textural interest of a good rough-cut marmalade. Curry, which is such a great companion for citrus, plays a starring role here.

pickled-beet
CARPACCIO
WITH HONEY & THYME

AN EYE-CATCHING READY-MADE APPETIZER

I love to cook for people, but my entertaining skills can leave something to be desired. I can easily get lost in what I'm preparing and, before I know it, 4 hours have passed and I have hungry, grumpy people on my hands. Part of my problem is I don't give enough attention to premeal snacks, which are all but necessary when you have a tendency, like I do, to get lost in what you're cooking.

So, when I was developing the pickle recipes for this book, I had in mind the possibility of making something that was more or less a ready-made appetizer—something that went beyond just snacking on pickles out of the jar—and this recipe was born. I strain and reserve the brine and arrange these slices on a plate sprinkled with whatever cheese I have on hand (goat cheese is especially nice) and maybe some toasted pumpkin or sesame seeds for crunch. Of course, because they're thinly sliced, these have excellent sandwich potential as well.

INGREDIENTS

1½ pounds beets (about 3 large), scrubbed and greens removed

1½ cups apple cider vinegar

½ cup water

¼ cup honey

¼ teaspoon salt

FOR EACH JAR:

1 crushed clove garlic

2 sprigs fresh thyme

MATERIALS

Basic supplies for vinegar preserves (see page 78)

Rimmed baking sheet

Foil

Yield: 2 pints

1. Preheat the oven to 400°F. Leave the beets whole unless they vary greatly in size. Cut any very large beets in half to ensure even cooking.

2. Make a foil packet around the beets and place it on a baking sheet.

3. Roast the beets for 1 hour or until a knife inserted into the flesh doesn't meet any resistance.

4. Once the beets are done, open the foil packet and let them cool until they're no longer too hot to handle. At this point, use your fingers to rub the skins off the beets. They should readily come off.

5. Use a mandoline or knife to slice the beets ⅛ inch thick.

6. Combine the vinegar, water, honey, and salt in a medium saucepan.

7. Over high heat, stir the mixture to dissolve the salt and honey. Once the salt and honey are dissolved, add the beets and bring everything to a boil.

8. As soon as the brine comes to a boil, reduce the heat to low and simmer for 5 minutes. Remove from heat.

9. Place the garlic clove and thyme sprigs in each jar.

10. Ladle the beets into the prepared pint jars, evenly distributing them and then the brine, leaving ½-inch headspace. Remove air bubbles and wipe rims. Place the lids on the jars and screw on the bands until they are fingertip tight.

11. Process in a water-bath canner for 30 minutes, adjusting for altitude if needed.

12. After 24 hours, check the seals. Label, date, and store out of direct sunlight without the bands for up to a year.

INGREDIENTS

1 pound 12 ounces (about 8 medium) black plums, pitted and roughly chopped

¾ cup sugar

¾ cup apple cider vinegar

1 tablespoon ground mustard

2 tablespoons whole yellow mustard seed

3 turns ground black pepper

¼ teaspoon crushed red pepper

2 tablespoons maple syrup

MATERIALS

Basic supplies for vinegar preserves (see page XX)

Immersion blender

Yield: about 3 half pints

1. Combine the plums, sugar, and vinegar in a medium saucepan. Bring to a boil over high heat.

2. As soon as the plums begin to soften, after about 5 minutes, remove the mixture from the heat and carefully puree with an immersion blender. It doesn't need to be a completely homogenous purée; some small pieces of visible peel are fine and will add texture.

3. After puréeing, add ground and whole mustard seeds, black pepper, crushed red pepper, and maple syrup.

4. Return the mixture to a simmer for about 15 more minutes, until it has reduced slightly and mustard seeds have begun to soften.

5. Ladle into prepared half-pint jars, leaving ½-inch headspace. Remove air bubbles and wipe rims. Place the lids on the jars and screw on the bands until they're fingertip tight.

6. Process in a water-bath canner for 10 minutes, adjusting for altitude if needed.

7. After 24 hours, check the seals. Label, date, and store out of direct sunlight without the bands for up to a year.

maple-plum MOSTARDA

A SAVORY PLUM SAUCE WITH A MUSTARDY BITE

Traditionally, a mostarda is an Italian condiment made of candied fruit in a mustard-spiked syrup. Here, I'm using the term very loosely to describe this sweet, sour, mustardy plum sauce. Sort of like a pared down chutney that focuses on the mustard, this versatile sauce is as at home on a cheese tray as it is with roasts.

There's no need to peel the plums here as the whole mixture gets puréed early on in the process. I used a black freestone plum for this, meaning the pit (the stone) detaches freely from the flesh. If you end up with a clingstone variety, halve the plum, hold it right over your cooking saucepan, and use your hands to smoosh all the flesh away from the stone. That way, you won't lose any juice or flesh.

bloody mary PICKLED EGGS

FEATURING A BLOODY MARY–INSPIRED BRINE WITH HORSERADISH, CELERY SALT, AND SPICE

There's a certain level of one-upmanship that goes into bloody mary garnishes: seven kinds of pickles, a tiny hamburger—you get the idea. This pickled-egg recipe was inspired by just such a bloody mary recipe, which on the menu was rather unassuming, but arrived at the table dressed with a hardboiled egg, bacon, olives, and an entire rib of celery. As a cocktail garnish, the egg was a little cumbersome, but in terms of flavor, I thought the combination was right on.

A quart mason jar is an ideal vessel for this pickle, but I've included a bit of extra brine in case you prefer to use a different shape jar or split this up into smaller vessels, because it's important that the eggs are completely covered with the brine. You can squish them down, but not enough to split them. Impressively enough, about a dozen hard-boiled eggs will fit in a quart mason jar.

INGREDIENTS

1 dozen eggs
1 cup canned tomato sauce
1½ cups apple cider vinegar
1 teaspoon celery seed
1 tablespoon prepared horseradish
¼ teaspoon crushed red pepper
2 tablespoons sugar
¼ teaspoon salt, or more to taste
Freshly ground black pepper to taste

MATERIALS

Large nonreactive saucepan
Small nonreactive saucepan
Stockpot for sterilizing
Quart mason jar
Ice-water bath

--- *Yield: 1 quart, or about 1 dozen pickled eggs* ---

1. In a large nonreactive saucepan, cover the eggs with water by 1 inch. Bring to a boil over high heat and boil for 10 minutes.

2. Plunge the eggs into a bath of icy water and let cool completely before peeling. Peel the eggs and pack them in a still-warm, sterilized quart jar. To sterilize a quart jar, bring it to a full rolling boil it in a water bath and boil for 10 minutes.

3. Whisk together the tomato sauce, vinegar, celery seed, horseradish, crushed red pepper, sugar, salt, and black pepper in a small saucepan. Bring the mixture to a boil over high heat.

4. Once the mixture boils, reduce the heat to low and simmer for 5 minutes.

5. Pour the brine over the eggs so that they are completely covered. Store in the fridge.

6. Let the eggs cure in the fridge for at least a few days before consuming. They'll get better the longer they sit in the brine and will last in the fridge about a month. *This recipe cannot be safely processed in a water-bath canner.*

INGREDIENTS

1 pound poblano peppers (about 3 large peppers), or enough to produce 2½ cups after grinding

1 pound Anaheim chiles (about 4 chiles), or enough to produce 2½ cups after grinding

1½ cups cider vinegar

1½ cups sugar

1½ teaspoons salt

MATERIALS

Basic supplies for vinegar preserves (see page 78)

Food processor

green chile JAM

A SWEET, SOUR, AND MILDLY SPICY JAM

Here in the Southwest, green chile is serious business. Green chile can refer to a sauce made from green chiles or the dish smothered in that sauce. If someone says the plural, "green chiles," they're probably talking about the produce itself, sold on the side of the road roasted or fresh in late summer. Those that originate in Hatch, New Mexico, known as Hatch chiles, are the most notorious.

In this recipe, I use a combination of the more widely available Anaheim chiles and poblanos for this sweet-and-sour chile jam with just a little bit of heat. Poblanos can vary in heat pretty greatly, so taste a bit before you go ahead with this recipe. If they're on the spicy side, seed them before proceeding. If they're not too spicy for your liking, save yourself the trouble and leave the seeds in; they'll lend the final product a nice bit of heat.

Yield: about 4 half pints

1. Roughly chop the poblanos, then pulse them in a food processor until ground. They should be very finely chopped, but not puréed. Measure 2½ cups of the poblanos and their juice. Repeat with the Anaheim chiles.

2. Combine the ground peppers and chiles, cider vinegar, sugar, and salt in your preserving pot and bring the mixture to a boil over high heat.

3. Once the mixture boils, reduce the heat to low and simmer for 30 minutes.

4. Ladle into prepared half-pint jars, leaving ½-inch headspace. Remove air bubbles and wipe rims. Place the lids on the jars and screw on the bands until they're fingertip tight.

5. Process in a water-bath canner for 10 minutes, adjusting for altitude if needed.

6. After 24 hours, check the seals. Label, date, and store out of direct sunlight without the bands for up to a year.

quick pickled RHUBARB

A FRIDGE PICKLE THAT PRESERVES THE TART FLAVOR AND TEXTURE OF FRESH RHUBARB

The first time I brought home rhubarb from the market after my boyfriend and I moved in together, I was pretty startled when he walked over to the cutting board as I was chopping and popped some in his mouth raw. Let's just say I had some questions. I learned that he often ate rhubarb raw as a kid by dipping it in sugar. I have to admit, in the midst of my love for cooking rhubarb into preserves, pies, and other sweet treats, I had completely overlooked its merits when raw.

There are a few reasons why rhubarb is best as a quick, fridge pickle. First, as we know from making chutney, rhubarb breaks apart readily almost as soon as it is heated. Processing this pickle in a water bath would compromise the crispy rhubarb. To preserve the pleasing crunch of the uncooked rhubarb, we're packing the raw slices into a pint mason jar, covering it with hot brine, then letting it cure in the fridge for about a week. This preserves the delicate flavor and crispy texture of raw rhubarb, while still producing a puckery, versatile pickle.

INGREDIENTS

6 ounces rhubarb sliced ½ inch thick, enough to fill a pint jar

½ cup apple cider vinegar

½ cup water

3 tablespoons sugar

Pinch salt

MATERIALS

Small stainless steel saucepan

Pint jar with 2-piece closure

Yield: about 1 pint

1. Fill a pint jar to the shoulder with rhubarb slices. You can shake the jar side to side to help fit more pieces, but do not pack them.

2. Bring the vinegar, water, sugar, and salt to a boil, stirring to dissolve the salt and sugar.

3. Once the brine boils (it won't take long), carefully pour the hot brine into the jar over the rhubarb slices.

4. Let cool to room temperature, cover with a 2-piece mason jar lid, label, and refrigerate. Wait 1 week before eating, if you can help it, to allow the pickle to cure.

spring radish & PICKLED RHUBARB PICO DE GALLO

A SPRING VEGETABLE PICO TO TIDE YOU OVER UNTIL TOMATO SEASON

Short of using them as a vehicle for butter, chopping them fine and stirring them into a simple salad or salsa is one of my favorite uses of radishes. When they start showing up at the greenmarket, tomatoes are still months away, but I'm craving something fresh on pretty much everything I put in my mouth. This highly nontraditional pico de gallo, featuring the spring greenmarket trifecta—scallions, radishes, and rhubarb—is the answer to that.

Although Quick Pickled Rhubarb (page 102) gives this a good amount of acid, lime juice provides tartness here and pulls everything together. Typically, a pico de gallo would have a fresh, hot pepper like a serrano or jalapeño, but to keep this as seasonal as possible, we'll stick to ground cayenne.

INGREDIENTS

2 cups finely chopped red radishes

½ cup Quick Pickled Rhubarb (page 102), finely chopped

½ cup scallion tops, thinly sliced

1 tablespoon lime juice

1 clove garlic, finely minced

Salt to taste

Cayenne to taste

Serves 4 as an appetizer

1. Stir together the radishes, rhubarb, scallions, lime juice, and garlic in a medium bowl.

2. Add salt and cayenne to taste and serve.

INGREDIENTS

4 ripe bananas

1 tablespoon grated fresh ginger, lightly packed

⅓ cup apple cider vinegar

⅓ cup plus 2 tablespoons sugar

¼ teaspoon crushed red pepper

2 teaspoons onion powder

¼ teaspoon ground allspice

¼ teaspoon ground cloves

Salt to taste

MATERIALS

Medium stainless steel saucepan

Immersion blender

Pint mason jar

Yield: 1 scant pint

1. Peel the bananas and break them into ½-inch chunks with your hands as you add them to the saucepan. Add the ginger, apple cider vinegar, and sugar.

2. Cook the banana mixture over medium-heat, just until simmering. Remove from the heat and carefully purée using an immersion blender until completely smooth.

3. Stir in the crushed red pepper, onion powder, allspice, and clove.

4. Return to low heat and cook for 20 minutes, stirring frequently, or until thickened. Add salt to taste.

5. Let cool to room temperature, transfer to a pint mason jar, label, and cover with a 2-piece mason jar lid. Store in the fridge. *This recipe cannot be safely processed in a water-bath canner.*

banana KETCHUP

A GINGERY ALL-PURPOSE CONDIMENT THAT PROVIDES A SAVORY USE FOR RIPE BANANAS

Also known as banana sauce, banana ketchup is a condiment popular in Filipino cuisine. It came to be out of necessity during World War II, when there was a shortage of tomatoes and, thus, tomato ketchup. Bananas were relatively abundant and banana ketchup was born. It was even dyed red to resemble tomato ketchup and remains an indispensable condiment in Filipino cooking today.

Now, I won't be so bold as to dis banana bread, but what excites me about banana ketchup is that it's not only delicious but it provides a savory option for using up overripe bananas stat. In many commercial versions of banana ketchup, the flavor of bananas doesn't make it through to the finished product. I wanted a more natural take that nixed the artificial coloring and let the flavor of banana shine through while still providing a very ketchuplike condiment. I am a ketchup fanatic, and I am happy to add this recipe to my repertoire.

INGREDIENTS

2 cups chopped cabbage, about ¼-inch pieces

1½ cups chopped cauliflower, about ¼-inch pieces

1 cup chopped tomatillos, about ¼-inch pieces

1 cup chopped white onions, about ¼-inch pieces

1 cup chopped poblano peppers, about ¼-inch pieces

1½ teaspoons salt

1¾ cups distilled white vinegar

¾ cup sugar

1 teaspoon whole yellow mustard seed

1 teaspoon ground mustard

½ teaspoon turmeric

MATERIALS

Basic supplies for vinegar preserves (see page 78)

Medium nonreactive bowl

=== Yield: 2 pints ===

southwest
CHOW-CHOW

A SPICY, SOUTHWEST-INSPIRED TAKE ON THE CLASSIC SOUTHERN RELISH

Chow-chow is a mustardy, end-of-season relish, meant to be a bit of a catchall for what has to be pulled from the garden before temperatures drop. Green tomatoes often make an appearance, as does cabbage. Because it has its roots in utility, there are as many versions of chow-chow as there are folks who make it. This one has a Southwest bent and includes poblanos in place of sweet green or red peppers, cauliflower, and tomatillos instead of green tomatoes.

This recipe takes just a bit of planning, as it needs to be salted and allowed to sit for 4 hours before going into jars. If you start it on a weekend morning when you wake up, it will be ready to process after lunch.

1. In a large bowl, use a wooden spoon to stir together the chopped cabbage, cauliflower, tomatillos, onions, poblano peppers, and sea salt. Let the mixture sit for 4 hours, during which time the salt will draw moisture out of the vegetables.

2. After 4 hours, take the chopped vegetables a handful at a time and squeeze them to extract as much liquid as possible. Do not rinse. Reserve the squeezed veggies in a medium nonreactive bowl.

3. Combine the vinegar, sugar, mustard seed, ground mustard, and turmeric in the stainless saucepan and bring to a boil over high heat. Stir to dissolve the sugar and salt.

4. Once the sugar and salt are dissolved, add the vegetables and return to a boil.

5. Reduce heat and simmer for 10 minutes.

6. Remove from the heat and use a slotted spoon to transfer the relish to the prepared jars. Pour the brine over the relish to cover, leaving ½-inch headspace. Remove air bubbles and wipe rims. Place the lids on the jars and screw on the bands until they're fingertip tight.

7. Process in a water-bath canner for 10 minutes, adjusting for altitude if needed.

8. After 24 hours, check the seals. Label, date, and store out of direct sunlight without the bands for up to a year.

old bay
PICKLED
CAULIFLOWER

THE CULT-FAVORITE SEASONING IS AS GOOD ON PICKLED CAULIFLOWER AS IT IS ON CRAB

Cauliflower was one of the first vegetables I ever pickled. I remember making a spicy pickled cauliflower recipe from Eugenia Bone's great book *Well-Preserved*. As in this recipe, it was a small batch; I think the yield was maybe 3 pints, and it disappeared much more quickly than my boyfriend and I expected. It was such a hit that we made another 2 batches and gave them with Christmas gifts that year.

Cauliflower is sort of the tofu of the vegetable world—although it has a reputation for being bland, if treated well, with lots of flavor, it's delicious. It's the perfect blank slate for bold flavors, so I paired it with Old Bay, the put-it-on-everything seafood flavoring with a cult following. There's no need to add additional salt to the brine because the Old Bay provides all the salt you need.

INGREDIENTS

14 ounces chopped cauliflower florets, about ¼-inch pieces

2 teaspoons Old Bay seasoning

¼ small white onion, thinly sliced

2 cups distilled white vinegar (5 percent)

½ cup sugar

MATERIALS

Basic supplies for vinegar preserves (see page 78)

Colander

Yield: 2 pints

1. Bring a medium saucepan of water to a boil and add the cauliflower. Once it returns to a boil, begin timing and boil the cauliflower for 3 minutes.

2. After 3 minutes, drain and discard the cooking water and set the cauliflower aside to cool.

3. Add 1 teaspoon of Old Bay to each prepared pint jar and divide the onion slices evenly between the 2 jars.

4. Divide the cauliflower florets evenly between the 2 jars.

5. Bring the vinegar and sugar to a boil, stirring to help the sugar dissolve.

6. Once the brine comes to a boil, pour it into the jars to cover the cauliflower, leaving ½-inch headspace. Remove air bubbles and wipe rims. Place the lids on the jars and screw on the bands until they're fingertip tight.

7. Process in a water-bath canner for 10 minutes, adjusting for altitude if needed.

8. After 24 hours, check the seals. Label, date, and store out of direct sunlight without the bands for up to a year.

INGREDIENTS

2 cups apple cider vinegar

1½ pounds apples (about 4 medium apples), cored and peeled

½ cup chopped white onion

½ teaspoon crushed red pepper

1 cup yellow raisins

2 cups brown sugar, loosely packed

2 tablespoons whole yellow mustard seed

2 tablespoons ground five-spice mixture (salt-free)

1 teaspoon salt

MATERIALS

Basic supplies for vinegar preserves (see page 78)

Yield: 3 half pints and 1 quarter pint

1. Pour the vinegar into your preserving pot.

2. Cut the apples into ¼-inch chunks and add to the pot as you cut them.

3. Add the remaining ingredients to the pot and bring to a boil over high heat.

4. Reduce heat to simmer and cook for about 45 minutes, or until the mixture thickens and the apple chunks become translucent.

5. Ladle into prepared half- and quarter-pint jars, leaving ½-inch headspace. Remove air bubbles and wipe rims. Place the lids on the jars and screw on the bands until they're fingertip tight.

6. Process in a water-bath canner for 15 minutes, adjusting for altitude if needed.

7. After 24 hours, check the seals. Label, date, and store out of direct sunlight without the bands for up to a year.

five-spice APPLE CHUTNEY

HIGHLIGHTING THE SAVORY SIDE OF APPLES WITH CHINESE FIVE SPICE

Chinese five-spice blend typically includes star anise, clove, cinnamon, fennel seed, and pepper. Sichuan pepper is traditional, but many Americanized versions use white pepper instead. Although it is traditionally used on rich meats like duck and pork, the warm spices make it an unexpected foil for fall fruits like apples. The fennel seed and pepper play up the savory side of the familiar fruits, making them perfect for a sweet-sour condiment like chutney.

If you can find them, select a firm-fleshed variety of apple that will mostly stand up to the cooking process. In general, tart varieties have firmer flesh. A less firm apple won't ruin the chutney, but it will produce a more jamlike texture.

DOUBLE-TART CHERRY RELISH *with cloves*

A FRUIT-BASED RELISH WITH LAYERED CHERRY FLAVOR

Perhaps you've noticed a lack of raisins in this book, sort of a rarity for a preserving volume. I guess it's time I explained. It's not that I hate them—unless they're in oatmeal cookies, where I'd argue they have *no place*—they're just not my first choice. I snuck yellow raisins into the Five-Spice Apple Chutney recipe on page 111 because I find them to be much more subtle and infinitely more pleasing than plain old brown raisins. In this recipe, inspired by the great Linda Ziedrich, I decided to bypass raisins by doubling up on tart cherry flavor.

The relish is somewhere between a mostarda and a chutney. We're skipping the savory add-ins like onion here to let the fruit shine, so it's not quite a chutney. It has a lot in common with a mostarda, minus the mustardy heat. It's tart, sweet, and gets a savory kick from the clove and black pepper. If you enjoy a smear of cranberry sauce on your turkey sandwich, then this one's for you.

INGREDIENTS

1 pound pitted fresh sour cherries (about 4 cups)

½ cup apple cider vinegar

1 cup sugar

¾ cup dried tart cherries, roughly chopped

½ teaspoon ground cloves

¼ teaspoon freshly ground black pepper

1 bay leaf

1 cinnamon stick

MATERIALS

Basic supplies for vinegar preserves (see page 78)

─────── *Yield: 2 half pints* ───────

1. Bring the fresh cherries, vinegar, and sugar to a boil over high heat.

2. Once the mixture boils, remove it from the heat and carefully use a potato masher to break down the cherries. You don't want a mush, just a very chunky purée in which there are no more whole cherries.

3. Add the dried cherries, ground cloves, ground pepper, bay leaf, and cinnamon stick to the pot and return to a boil over high heat.

4. Reduce heat and simmer for about 20 minutes, or until the mixture reduces and thickens slightly. Remove the cinnamon stick and bay leaf.

5. Ladle into prepared half-pint jars, leaving ½-inch headspace. Remove air bubbles and wipe rims. Place the lids on the jars and screw on the bands until they're fingertip tight.

6. Process in a water-bath canner for 10 minutes, adjusting for altitude if needed.

7. After 24 hours, check the seals. Label, date, and store out of direct sunlight without the bands for up to a year.

INGREDIENTS

2 pounds fresh figs (about 18 medium)

2 cups apple cider vinegar

2 cups sugar

½ cup ruby port

3 bay leaves

Pinch of salt

FOR EACH JAR:

10 black peppercorns

MATERIALS

Basic supplies for vinegar preserves (see page 78)

Yield: 2 pints

1. Cover the figs with water and bring to a boil over high heat. Reduce heat and simmer the figs for 15 minutes. Carefully drain the figs, discarding the cooking water.

2. Over high heat, stir the vinegar, sugar, port, bay leaves, and the pinch of salt until the sugar is dissolved. Add the figs and continue heating to bring the mixture to a boil.

3. Reduce heat and simmer for about 1 hour, stirring periodically.

4. Place 10 black peppercorns into each prepared jar.

5. Use a slotted spoon to evenly divide the figs between 2 pint jars. Pour the brine over the figs to cover, leaving ½-inch headspace. Remove air bubbles and wipe rims. Place the lids on the jars and screw on the bands until they're fingertip tight.

6. Process in a water-bath canner for 15 minutes, adjusting for altitude if needed.

7. After 24 hours, check the seals. Label, date, and store out of direct sunlight without the bands for up to a year.

PICKLED FIGS WITH PORT *& black pepper*

AN ELEGANT, PIQUANT WHOLE-FRUIT PICKLE

Although undoubtedly sweet, figs also have a savory quality that lends itself very well to pickles. You'll likely slice or chop them up for serving, but leaving the figs whole for pickling has an aesthetic and practical purpose—it keeps them from turning to mush. They'll be quite soft after the initial boil but will firm up as they're stewed in the vinegar syrup, becoming slightly candied. Just as the figs are beginning to cook in the brine, carefully puncture each one with a fork. This will allow the flavor of the brine to permeate the fruit as it cooks and will help reduce fruit float.

These pair well with all manner of rich, creamy cheeses, as their tartness and the sweetness of the port is a great complement.

smoky CARROT COINS

AN INTRIGUING BUT EASY COLD-PACK PICKLE

I am little picky when it comes to carrots. Carrot cake, not too surprisingly, is a yes. Carrots sticks are usually a no, but that can be changed with a decent dip. Basically, if I'm not aware that I'm consuming a carrot, I'm good. But roasted carrots are a resounding yes, so I set out to replicate their smoky flavor in this pickle, which I'll happily eat.

Unlike the Pizza-Pickled Brussels Sprouts (page 120), this is a cold-pack pickle. That means the carrots are not cooked before they're bathed in brine. It's nice because it means one less step, and the carrots are in small enough pieces that the heat from processing softens them sufficiently. My friend Tricia once passed along some serious kitchen wisdom to me: everything is better when it's cut on a bias. So, we're slicing our carrot coins about ¼ inch thick on a bias for this one because it's better.

INGREDIENTS

½ teaspoon each of whole yellow mustard seed, fennel seed, celery seed, smoked paprika, and crushed red pepper

1 pound carrots, peeled and cut into ¼-inch-thick coins

2 ½ cups apple cider vinegar

½ cup sugar

½ teaspoon salt

MATERIALS

Basic supplies for vinegar preserves (see page 78)

Yield: 2 pints

1. Place ¼ teaspoon each of whole yellow mustard seed, fennel seed, celery seed, smoked paprika, and crushed red pepper in each prepared pint jar.

2. Divide the peeled and prepped carrots between the 2 jars. You can shake them from side to side to help the contents settle.

3. Bring the vinegar, sugar, and salt to a boil over high heat, stirring to dissolve the sugar and salt.

4. Pour into prepared pint jars, leaving ½-inch headspace. Wipe rims. Place the lids on the jars and screw on the bands until they're fingertip tight.

5. Process in a water-bath canner for 15 minutes, adjusting for altitude if needed.

6. After 24 hours, check the seals. Label, date, and store out of direct sunlight without the bands for up to a year.

INGREDIENTS

1 cup apple cider vinegar

1 cup honey

1 cup fresh raspberries

Pinch salt

MATERIALS

Basic supplies for vinegar preserves (see page 78)

Yield: 2 half pints

1. Measure the vinegar and set it aside before you start cooking the honey. Over medium-low heat, cook the honey in a medium saucepan until it darkens noticeably, about 6 minutes.

2. Carefully stir the vinegar into the hot honey. The honey will sputter a bit. Stir in a pinch of salt.

3. Add the raspberries and return the mixture to a simmer over medium-low heat.

4. Reduce heat to low and simmer until the berries break apart and the mixture reduces slightly, about 10 minutes.

5. Use a fine mesh strainer to strain the liquid into a Pyrex measuring cup for easy pouring.

6. Pour into prepared half or quarter-pint jars, leaving ½-inch headspace. Wipe rims. Place the lids on the jars and screw on the bands until they're fingertip tight.

7. Process in a water-bath canner for 10 minutes, adjusting for altitude if needed.

8. After 24 hours, check the seals. Label, date, and store out of direct sunlight without the bands for up to a year.

raspberry & BURNT-HONEY GASTRIQUE

FEATURING A CONCENTRATED VINEGAR SAUCE WITH EARTHY DEPTH

"Burnt" honey, which is not really burnt but cooked until it darkens and caramelizes, is one of my favorite culinary tricks. Easier and less scary than making caramel from sugar, it's a quick way to add sweet, earthy depth to just about anything.

A *gastrique* is basically a concentrated, fruity, vinegar-based sauce, and it's incredibly versatile. I like to use it as an easy way to spruce up roast meats. If you want to get fancy, you can dribble or pool some on a plate before serving. I was superintrigued to find a couple of gastrique recipes for water-bath canning in Sherri Brooks Vinton's book *Put 'Em Up Fruit*. I quickly made one of them and the jars didn't last long in my larder, which is always a good sign.

If you're not up for canning this gastrique, you don't have to. It's quite a small batch and because of the amount of vinegar, it will keep for a substantial amount of time in the fridge. I like to save fridge space and can this one, however, because it's especially satisfying to pull a quarter pint of this off the shelf and immediately make dinner better.

PIZZA-PICKLED BRUSSELS SPROUTS

A FAVORITE WINTER VEGETABLE PICKLED WITH CLASSIC PIZZA SPICES

I'm not too particular when it comes to pizza toppings. I can't eat gluten, and I spent years trying to nail down a gluten-free pizza recipe that I loved and was easy to make. So when it was time to put on the toppings, my feeling was, more or less, anything goes. That said, I really love brussels sprouts, especially on pizza. So a brussels sprouts pickle, which infuses my favorite pizza topping with garlic, oregano, and crushed red pepper, was a no-brainer.

Selecting small sprouts for this pickle eliminates the need to cut them. Peel off any rough or discolored outer leaves, then trim the bottom of the sprout if needed, leaving as much as the stem intact as possible. This will help keep the sprouts from separating as they blanch and will ensure your final product is as pretty as it is delicious.

INGREDIENTS

14 ounces small brussels sprouts, outer leaves removed

2 cloves garlic, crushed

2 sprig freshs oregano

½ teaspoon crushed red pepper

2½ cups distilled white vinegar

½ cup sugar

½ teaspoon salt

MATERIALS

Basic supplies for vinegar preserves (see page 78)

Colander

Yield: 2 pints

1. Bring a medium sauccpan of water to a boil and add the Brussels sprouts. Once it returns to a boil, begin timing and boil the sprouts for 4 minutes.

2. After 4 minutes, drain and discard the cooking water and set the sprouts aside to cool.

3. Add 1 crushed garlic clove, 1 sprig of fresh oregano, and ¼ teaspoon of crushed red pepper to each jar.

4. Once they're cool enough to touch, but not cold, divide the sprouts evenly between the two jars.

5. Bring the vinegar, sugar, and salt to a boil, stirring to help the sugar and salt dissolve.

6. Once the brine comes to a boil, pour it into the jars to cover the sprouts, leaving ½-inch headspace. Remove air bubbles and wipe rims. Place the lids on the jars and screw on the bands until they're fingertip tight.

7. Process in a water-bath canner for 10 minutes, adjusting for altitude if needed.

8. After 24 hours, check the seals. Label, date, and store out of direct sunlight without the bands for up to a year.

FERMENTATION

IN SOME WAYS, FERMENTATION, LIKE WATER-bath canning, has been saddled with the reputation of requiring a lot of time, special equipment, and a mountain of cabbage. This couldn't be further from the truth. You can get started fermenting today with stuff you already have. Really.

Because it is, after all, a method of food preservation, fermentation can be used to extend the life of a large amount of produce at once, including, say, that mountain of cabbage. I find it's most practical, however, for the home cook to start on a smaller scale, so all the recipes in this chapter are scaled to fit in a quart mason jar. That way, those three rutabagas in your CSA box are plenty for a weekend fermentation project. Then, when you fall in love with a recipe for *curtido* with lime zest (page 158) like I did or have a week when your CSA box is *only* rutabagas, you have the know-how necessary to scale up.

There are as many methods and types of fermentation as there are those who practice it. Looking at each of them, even superficially, is beyond the scope of this book. Here, we're carving out our own niche, so in addition to zooming in on small-batch fermentation, we're also focusing only on lacto-fermentation. (Lacto-fermentation requires no starters or special ingredients beyond produce and salt.)

I started canning long before I started down the path that left me smitten with fermentation. Perhaps that's why the aspect of fermentation I want most to emphasize is *play*. I worked in an elementary school for 4 years and I can almost picture the smooshing of salt and vegetables required for fermentation as something the kindergartners might do. Because the physical work of fermentation is quite tactile and fun, and because there is so much room for experimentation while producing a safe product, I think of fermentation as the preserver's place to play. This is a cookbook, so there are recipes to come, but I also encourage you to use the simple ratios that follow to create your own fermented vegetables as well. Many of the recipes that follow are "kraut-chis," to borrow a term from Sandor Ellix Katz in *The Art of Fermentation*, sauerkraut-kimchi hybrids that resulted from just this sort of experimentation.

THE VEGETABLES

Almost all the recipes in this chapter involve fermenting vegetables, but a couple of kimchis incorporate fruit. Of the three methods—sweet preserves, pickles, and fermentation—I prioritize the use of organic or unsprayed produce the highest in fermentation. Conventional produce can be treated with preservatives in addition to pesticides, which can actually inhibit fermentation. Furthermore, because it's best to leave the skin on vegetables you're going to ferment to include any beneficial naturally occurring microbes on the vegetables, organic or unsprayed is safest.

Again, do what you can. I live in a small, rural town and can appreciate that not everyone has ready access to organic daikon. Can you ferment conventional produce? Sure. I have and do, but I strive to select organic and/or unsprayed vegetables when I can. In fact, if you have a ferment on your hands that isn't successful and you can't pinpoint why, conventional produce could be the culprit. (I had a series of ferments that weren't doing anything, and I came to suspect that their shared ingredient, the same knob of conventional horseradish, was to blame.)

There's a reason why so many fermented vegetable recipes contain fall and winter vegetables: they ferment so darn well and the timing is right! Cabbages, radishes, turnips, rutabagas, beets, and parsnips make excellent ferments. Traditionally, fermenting vegetables harvested at the end of the growing season served to extend the season. Plus, cooler fall and winter temperatures are ideal for producing a ferment that matures and develops its signature sour tang slowly, resulting in more depth of flavor. Finally, fermenting vegetables preserves their vitamin C and helps probiotics flourish, making them an ideal part of a winter diet in a cool-weather climate where not as many nutrient-rich foods are available locally during the winter months. However, late summer–harvested veggies like green beans and hot peppers ferment excellently in a brine. There isn't a vegetable that won't ferment, but some do better than others.

Vegetables that are a little wilty will still ferment fine, but be sure to cut out and remove any mold or soft spots. Unless you come across something particularly gnarly or rough, vegetables should not be peeled.

THE SALT

Just as you can use any vegetable to ferment, you can use any salt to ferment. However, some will produce better results than others. Although it is possible to use iodized salt in ferments, I do not recommend it. I recommend unrefined fine-grain sea salt or kosher salt, in that order. Sea salt does have advantages over kosher salt, as the fermentation process makes trace minerals in the salt bioavailable. Unrefined sea salt, however, can be harder to find, and kosher salt produces a great ferment. Truly, any type of salt can be used, but try to avoid those that contain anti-caking agents, which includes some kosher salts.

Because you can use any type of salt, the only accurate way to measure salt for ferments and—frankly—the easiest way, is to use weight rather than volume. For this reason, all the recipes in this chapter use grams (versus tablespoons, say) as a unit of measurement. The granule size of different types of salt varies greatly. Even among unrefined sea salts, there's incredible variation in the size of granules. This means that a tablespoon of finely ground sea salt is a very different amount of salt than a tablespoon of a coarser sea salt. Measuring the quantities of salt and produce for ferments in grams is not only easier, it ensures both success and accuracy.

Since fermentation allows for a greater amount of flexibility, it might seem counterintuitive to weigh out salt down to the gram. My intention is that using weight rather than volume will, in fact, help facilitate flexibility and simplify the prep process. For example, if you're making the Pink House Kraut on page 139 and have only one beet in the fridge, you can adjust the amount of salt needed by weighing the produce you have and calculating the proper ratio of salt. Similarly, if you want to increase a recipe to accommodate a bumper crop from last week's CSA, you can likewise weigh the total amount of produce and recalculate the proper amount of salt. Speaking more generally, my kitchen scale makes my preserving life so much easier. I suspect once you take the kitchen-scale plunge, you'll agree.

THE WATER

The elegant simplicity of fermentation is in part due to water and salt. And although it really is that simple, at the risk of overcomplicating things, the water you use matters, perhaps more so than any of the other ingredients in your ferment.

Chlorine, which is added to many municipal water supplies, can inhibit or prevent fermentation. Boiling water for twenty minutes can evaporate chlorine, but the water must be allowed to cool down to room temperature again before being used to ferment. Water can also be left out for a day or two in a bowl or pitcher with a large surface area so that chlorine will evaporate.

When I lived in New York City, I would ferment with tap water without a problem. Perhaps surprisingly to those who have never lived there, New York City has fantastic tap water. Where I live now, our city water is incredibly hard and is treated with chlorine to such a degree that one time I woke up and smelled bleach, half joked with my boyfriend that he had been cleaning all night, only to realize the smell was our tap water. Needless to say, we use filtered water. Therefore, all the recipes in the book were developed using filtered water. Unless you are sure it is not treated, I recommend you do the same or start with a very small test batch.

THE STUFF

Because by now you know that I'm a fan of experimenting with small batches and learning what I like, all the recipes in this chapter are small scale and written to be put up in quart mason jars. There are a truly impressive number of fermenting vessels and systems, but I'll focus on the quart mason jar because I believe it's an uncomplicated, accessible starting point.

Part one of this basic fermentation setup is a **wide-mouth quart mason jar**. A wide-mouth quart jar is best because, in many of the following recipes, you'll need to get produce in and out of the jar with ease. All of the ferments in this chapter are anaerobic, meaning they don't require access to oxygen. Technically, you could put a lid on these ferments throughout the fermentation process. This quickly solves the issue of keeping bugs out of your kraut, but it creates another variable: the buildup of gas inside the jar, especially during the early stages of the fermentation process. Rather than putting a lid on it, I prefer to use one of the many a simple **airlock systems** made specifically for small-batch fermentation in quart mason jars.

If I'm being honest, I have to say I wasn't originally an advocate of using an airlock system for small-batch fermentation. I'm very much in the the-less-I-have-to-buy-the-better camp. All those years of tiny-apartment living really did a number on me! I also felt that having to buy one more thing in order to start fermenting might be one more barrier for folks to trying fermentation, and that is certainly not what I want. That said, after fermenting with an airlock and seeing that it simplifies the process exponentially, nearly eliminates the potential for surface molds, and produces more consistent results, I am now confident in recommending it as the best option.

I now make all my ferments using these systems, which you can make very inexpensively or purchase online. A number of folks make airlock systems meant particularly for wide-mouth mason jars. These make it easy to attach an airlock to a specialized lid that allows carbon dioxide to escape as pressure builds but otherwise creates an airtight seal. As much as I appreciate the minimalism of fermentation, I cannot recommend mason jar airlock systems enough. Particularly for folks who are beginning fermenters, I think they can be a great tool to help build confidence. They also drastically cut down on the odor, which can be a big plus if you live with roommates or others who might not be as excited about fermentation as you are. (See the Resources section, page 187, for buying recommendations.) That said, an online search will reveal that there are numerous other fermentation setups. If you have a setup that you're already comfortable with and confident in, by all means use it.

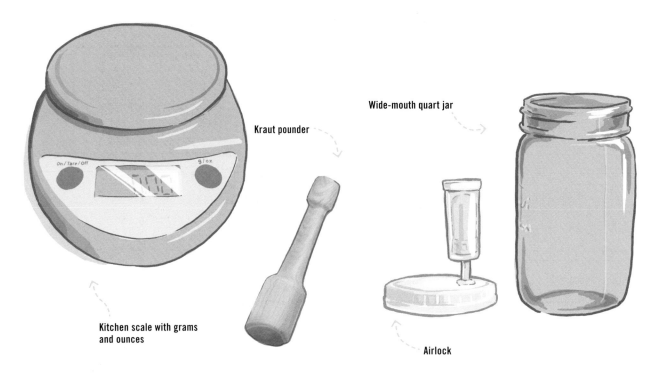

Kitchen scale with grams and ounces

Kraut pounder

Wide-mouth quart jar

Airlock

The only other essential piece of equipment required to create the recipes in this book that you may not already own is a **digital kitchen scale**. I know this can be a tender spot for people, but because it is easier, more accurate, and cuts down on prep time and the number of dishes you have to do, I urge you to make your next appliance purchase a simple kitchen scale that includes both grams and ounces. A basic one, like the model I used to develop all of the recipes in this book, costs under thirty dollars. If that's not in your budget anytime soon, borrow one from a friend or a kitchen tool share in your area. It will serve you far beyond the recipes in this chapter.

As far as the other nice-to-haves for lacto-fermentation, I do appreciate my **food processor** when it comes to quickly grating or slicing a large quantity of root

BASIC FERMENTING EQUIPMENT

You'll want to round up the following basic equipment before you get started:

- **Wide-mouth quart mason jars**
- **An airlock system designed for a wide-mouth quart mason jar**
- **A large nonreactive bowl**
- **A kitchen scale that has both grams and ounces**

- **A wooden spoon**
- **Something to weight the vegetables to keep them submerged (brining only)**

Use a small Weck jar lid to weight brined ferments

vegetables, but a **box grater** works well too. A **kraut pounder**, which looks like a tiny wooden bat, can be a useful tool in—surprise—pounding kraut and kimchis into jars, but your fist performs this function as well. There are also simple **glass and ceramic weights** made especially for wide-mouth quart jars. I use the glass lid of a small Weck jar. With an airlock, I weight my ferments only when I'm brining. Again, see the Resources section on page 187 for more information on these products.

THE PROCESS

The recipes that follow employ two possible fermentation techniques: dry salting or brining. Dry salting describes simply applying salt to the produce, which has been shredded or cut very thinly, drawing liquid out to form a brine of the salt and the produce's own juices. Brining describes dissolving salt in water to form a brine in which to submerge larger pieces of produce. Use dry salting for krauts, most kimchis, and all the kraut-chis in between when you're working with shredded, small, and/or thin pieces of produce. Use brining when you want to produce something that looks more like a vinegar pickle—think dilly beans and jalapeño slices—bigger pieces of produce in a brine.

   My general rule is that if a vegetable will produce its own brine, use it! It will be more flavorful than a simple salt brine. The amount of brine you get in a kraut recipe will depend on the produce you use. Squeeze as much liquid as you can out of the dry-salted vegetables, which, in my experience, typically will just cover the vegetables.

THE BASIC PROCESS FOR DRY SALTING

1. Place a large nonreactive bowl (glass and stainless work well) on top of your kitchen scale. Zero the scale. Add your shredded, grated, or thinly sliced vegetables to the bowl. Record the weight.

2. Calculate 1.5 percent of the total weight of your produce. The recommended amount of salt to use in dry-salted ferments is 1.5 to 2 percent. I always start with the lower amount. If it's summer and/or very hot where you're fermenting and you notice your ferments developing too quickly or becoming mushy, try 2 percent. I developed all the recipes in this book using a ratio of 1.5 percent salt to vegetables.

Step 3

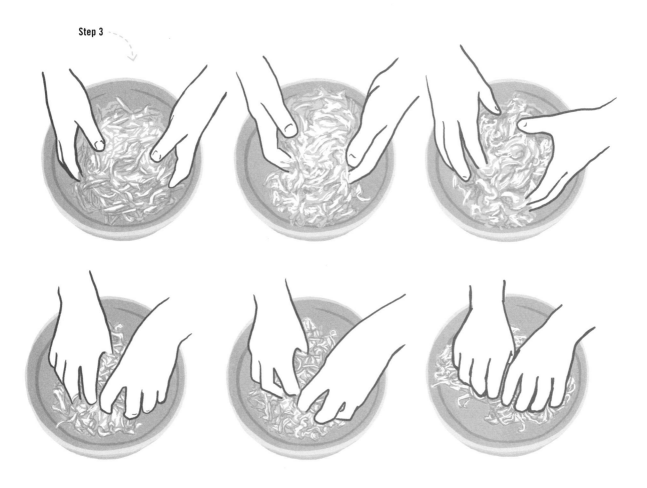

3. Zero the scale and add the salt to the vegetables in the bowl right on the scale. Remove the bowl from the scale and work the salt into the produce using your hands for about 2 minutes. Wash your hands first, but avoid antibacterial soap because it can work against the fermentation process. If you've ever "massaged" kale for a salad, that's the motion you want to employ here. In slightly less technical terms, it's basically smooshing. You'll begin to feel the vegetables wilt slightly and see a layer of liquid on the bottom on the bowl. It will also become much more difficult to detect the grains of salt.

4. Use your hands to pack the produce tightly into a quart mason jar. Put one handful in the jar, pack it down with your fist, put in another handful, and pack it down with your fist. Continue filling the jar in this manner until it is full just to the bottom of the jar shoulder. The back of a wooden spoon or a kraut pounder can help with this process as well.

5. At this point, the produce should be covered or just about covered with its own brine. When using an airlock for dry-salted ferments, I find that it is not necessary to weight the contents. Secure the ferment with an airlock system and leave at room temperature, out of direct sunlight, for the time indicated.

6. When the ferment is done, cover with a two-piece mason jar lid, date, label, and transfer to the refrigerator.

THE BASIC PROCESS FOR BRINING

1. Place a quart mason jar on your kitchen scale, zero the scale, and add water. Weigh the amount of water you'll use and record the weight. To brine a quart jar of vegetables, make a full quart of brine. You'll likely have leftovers, but because salt is a relatively inexpensive resource, it's better to make more brine than you need. If I end up with extra and have a few ferments going, I'll store it in the fridge for up to a week in a quart jar to top off active ferments as needed or experiment with a small-batch ferment using whatever I have on hand.

2. Calculate 5 percent of the weight of the water used and record this number. A 5 percent brine, in which the weight of the salt is 5 percent the weight of the water, is standard.

3. Zero the scale again and add the indicated amount of salt to the jar of water right on the scale. The water does not need to be warm to dissolve the salt. Place a lid on the jar and shake it until the salt is dissolved. That's it!

4. Place a separate, clean, dry quart mason jar on your scale. Zero the scale and measure the vegetables into the jar right on the scale.

5. Pour the brine over the vegetables so that the produce is fully submerged by at least 1 inch. Use your hands or a wooden chopstick to jostle the contents of the jar, releasing air bubbles.

6. Unless your airlock system has a weight built in, weight the contents so that the vegetables remain below the brine. I find that small Weck jar lids work particularly well for this, as do quarter-pint jars when there's enough space. Position the weight in the quart jar so that it holds the pieces of produce below the brine, leaving the weight in for the duration of the fermentation period. Secure the ferment with an airlock system.

7. When the ferment is done, cover with a two-piece mason jar lid, date, label, and transfer to the refrigerator.

FINDING YOUR FERMENTATION SPOT

When I lived in a roughly three-hundred-square-foot apartment in Queens, I always placed my ferments on a stool, directly inside the front door. One time, when the ferment of the moment was a gallon jar of kombucha, a friend was particularly startled upon entering my apartment and made a comment about how I had unwittingly invented a very effective burglar deterrent.

There was, however, a method to my madness. Generally, the best place for your ferments to live is one of the cooler spots in your home that is also out of direct sun. It should ideally also be a spot that isn't completely out of sight to facilitate your keeping an eye on your ferments, or at the very least noticing if something has gone awry when you pass by. In my Queens apartment, counter space was at a premium and my small kitchen heated up very quickly when the stove and oven were in use, hence the stool inside the front door instead. Now that I have a bit more counter space and my kitchen happens to be the coldest spot in my house, I keep my active ferments on my kitchen island.

VISITING YOUR KIMCHI AND OTHER TROUBLESHOOTING TIPS

Part of what I really love about fermentation is watching the food slowly transform. I rarely have enough self-control to not peek at my ferments at least once a day, and truly the best way to avoid any surprises with your fermentation projects is to visit them often. Look at them each day, begin tasting them when the initial burst of fermentation slows, and skim any scum off the surface using a clean spoon. Visiting and tasting them frequently will help you know when they're done.

And when are they done? Really, if you like how it tastes, then it's ready to eat! Because they're safe and edible throughout the fermentation process, readiness is pretty subjective when it comes to ferments. I know that might be a frustrating answer. For folks wanting more of a concrete benchmark, here's how I judge: when they taste more sour than salty, they're ready. I always pull a ferment and put it in the fridge as soon as I notice the texture declining, that is, getting mushy. Ideally, you won't get to the point of having a mushy ferment, unless of course you decide that's what you like.

Generally speaking, ferments will develop much slower in the winter because of cooler temperatures than they will in the summer. As you ferment more and more in your space throughout the year, you'll get a sense of how long things tend to take to get to a point where they've soured to your liking, and you will feel comfortable tasting things less frequently to gauge their progress.

The following are common occurrences you may encounter with small-batch fermentation and how to address them.

CLOUDY BRINE: That's a good thing! If your brine is cloudy, it means fermentation is happening. Particularly near the end of fermentation, the cloudiness of the brine can take the form of what looks like white, flaky bits. These are also normal and good and will likely settle to the bottom of your jar.

WHITE FILM/SCUM ON THE SURFACE OF THE BRINE: Kahm yeast is often to blame for the white film or scum that can form on the surface of the brine. It is not harmful, but some folks find it lends an undesirable taste to the finished product. If you see it, skim it!

BUBBLING: That's a good thing too! You may not get vigorous bubbling, but—especially al the beginning of fermentation—you are likely to notice bubbles and/or foam around your jar weight and on the surface of the ferment. Conversely, if you don't notice bubbles, don't despair.

MOLD: If you're checking your ferments regularly and skimming film when you notice it, mold should be a rare occurrence in these small-batch, relatively short-term ferments, especially if you're using an airlock. If you notice mold on a piece of vegetable that poked above the brine level accidentally or on the surface of the brine, simply use a clean spoon or paper towel to remove and discard it. As long as it remains on the surface, it's not cause for concern.

BUILDUP OF PRESSURE INSIDE JARS: Transferring a finished ferment to the fridge slows fermentation way, way down, but it doesn't stop it completely. If you take a ferment from the fridge, remove the lid, and pressure is released, that alone should not be cause for alarm.

TO STERILIZE OR NOT?

Do the jars need to be sterilized when you ferment? There are differing opinions on this. Since quart jars are much easier to sterilize than, say, a crock, if you're still getting comfortable with the idea of fermentation and it eases your nerves, by all means boil those jars for ten minutes and sterilize them. If it means you're more likely to feel comfortable eating the finished product, definitely sterilize. However, it is not absolutely necessary. The jars should be clean: washed with hot soapy water and allowed to dry thoroughly. Over the years, I have made successful ferments with unsterilized and sterilized jars but did not sterilize the jars when I tested any of the recipes for this book.

DO IT YOURSELF

I can't stress enough that one of the coolest parts of fermentation, for me, is the degree to which it allows for experimentation. Using the simple ratios and techniques for dry salting and brining described here, there is plenty of room for play. When I'm trying something new, my favorite bases—the vegetables that make up the majority of the ferment—are daikon and green cabbage. Turnips also work as a fairly neutral base. To those, you can add supplemental ingredients and flavors, like hot peppers, brussels sprouts, beets, onions, parsnips—the list goes on—in smaller amounts.

When I'm playing around with an ingredient that I haven't fermented before and I'm not entirely sure how it will behave, I usually add a little bit into a neutral base and experiment that way. Use fresh or dried herbs, citrus zest, and seaweeds to add flavor to your ferments.

Using a neutral base isn't the only way to experiment. There were many times when I was developing the recipes for this book that I was left with a hodgepodge of leftover root vegetables—something like one parsnip, one black radish, and a few carrots. I grated them up, added some salt, and saw what happened. Think of it as your new crisper-clean-out strategy. In my experience, sugary roots like parsnips and beets work best as supporting players, though, as do dark, leafy greens.

IS THIS HOW IT'S SUPPOSED TO SMELL?

The short answer is yes. I've been fermenting long enough that the smell of active ferments barely registers with me anymore. So, I was a bit startled when a friend told me that she had just tried making kimchi but had been discouraged and composted it because of the smell. Her boyfriend, with whom she shares a living space, confirmed: it really smelled. I told them that was a good thing! That means it is working.

I found her reaction completely understandable, though. We have instincts that make us leery of food with strong smells and, particularly in the early stages, when ferments are very active, the smell will be significant. If you or someone you live with is particularly bothered by the smell—or if you don't want to have to explain the odor to your guests—the mason jar airlocks described earlier are a fantastic way to very nearly eliminate the smell during the fermentation period. I loaned my kimchi-wary friends one of my mason jar airlock setups for their next ferment.

dilly BEANS

A RELIABLE BRINED PICKLE THAT TRANSLATES FROM WATER-BATH CANNING TO FERMENTING

Like corn relish, dilly beans are a classic in the water-bath canon. The traditional version is a vinegar pickle that typically consists of snappy green beans, plenty of garlic, and fresh dill. If you're lucky, you have a garden or a generous friend to provide a flowering dill head, which looks especially pretty while infusing the brine with the signature dill flavor.

Dilly beans are a water-bath canning recipe that translates beautifully to fermenting. Simply swap out the vinegar brine for a saltwater brine, and you can create a crisp, lacto-fermented pickled dilly bean. Because it can be a challenge to consistently produce a crispy texture when pickling cucumbers in a salt brine, dilly beans are my go-to, easy fermented pickle when I want a crunchy snack.

INGREDIENTS

1 garlic clove, sliced very thin

2 6-inch sprigs of fresh dill or 1 flowering dill head

285 grams green beans, ends trimmed

Enough 5 percent brine to cover by at least 1 inch

MATERIALS

Basic fermenting supplies (see page 128)

Yield: 1 scant quart

1. Place the slices of garlic clove and the dill in the bottom of a quart jar so that they lie flat. If you're using a flowering dill head, push it, stem end down, into the jar before adding the green beans to keep it looking pretty.

2. On top of the garlic and dill, stand the beans in the jar in a single layer, fitting them snugly side by side.

3. Pour the brine into the jar so it completely covers the vegetables. Use a wooden chopstick to jiggle the contents to help remove air bubbles. Unless your airlock system has a weight built in, weight the contents so that the vegetables remain below the brine. Seal the jar with an airlock system and allow to ferment at room temperature for up to 2 weeks. You may begin tasting for doneness after 3 days.

4. Cover, label, and refrigerate for long-term storage.

INGREDIENTS

340 grams red cabbage (about half a small head), thinly sliced on a mandoline or as thin as you can with a knife

180 grams daikon, thinly sliced on a mandoline or as thin as you can with a knife

170 grams red beet (about 2 small), thinly sliced on a mandoline, or grated

15 grams fresh unpeeled ginger, grated

11 grams salt

MATERIALS

Basic fermenting supplies (see page 128)

Mandoline, food processor, or box grater

Yield: 1 scant quart

1. In a large glass bowl, combine the cabbage, daikon, beets, ginger, and salt.

2. Use your hands to stir the ingredients together, then work the salt into the produce using your hands for about 2 minutes. If you've ever "massaged" kale for a salad, that's the motion you want to employ here. In slightly less technical terms, it's basically smooshing. The vegetables will begin releasing their liquid.

3. Use your hands to pack the produce tightly into a quart mason jar, one handful at a time.

4. Once the produce is packed in the jar, push it down with your fist, the back of a wooden spoon, or both, a few times.

5. Now the produce should be just about covered with its own brine.

6. Secure the jar with an airlock system and allow the kraut to ferment for up to 2 weeks. You may begin tasting for doneness after 3 days.

7. Cover, label, and refrigerate for long-term storage.

BEET SYRUP?

Beets that are more sugary—usually those that have been stored through cooler months—have a tendency to produce a brine that is thicker and, at times, syrupy. It's not harmful, but can be off-putting. If you're buying beets without the greens attached, it's a good indicator that they're more likely to have this effect. One way to counteract it is to increase the ratio of other vegetables to beets in a recipe.

PINK HOUSE KRAUT

A GINGERY RED CABBAGE KRAUT THAT'S THE PERFECT ADD-IN FOR ARUGULA

I've been captivated in recent years by the resurgence of using vegetable- and herb-based natural dyes for fabric. After witnessing the vibrant magenta color of this kraut, I can see why these plant-based dyes are gaining popularity again. The color of this kraut is truly stunning and if you're the sort to show some fermented love, this pretty red kraut is totally Valentine's Day material. Coincidentally, it is very nearly the color of my bright-pink house.

Here, a pretty standard kraut base of red cabbage is dressed up with red beets, radish, and ginger. Grated beets add earthiness to the mix, and the daikon adds funk (in a good way) and helps produce liquid for the brine. If you can't find daikon, plain red radishes will work here too. Use this wherever you use shaved red cabbage—I've mixed this into many an arugula-based salad.

WHITE KIMCHI

A NO-SPICE KIMCHI WITH ASIAN PEAR INSPIRED BY THE TRADITIONAL KOREAN *MUL KIMCHI*

Although in American popular food culture, kimchi is probably most commonly associated with spice, there are numerous of types of kimchi, many of them not at all spicy. This white kimchi, made with napa cabbage, Korean radish, Asian pear, garlic, and ginger, is perfect to make in the fall, when most of the ingredients are available in greenmarkets. Korean radish is a shorter, stouter relative of daikon, but if you can't find it, daikon is a fine substitution.

A variation on the brothy, cooling *Mul Kimchi* (water kimchi), this is brined rather than dry salted. It is also a bit milder and should be allowed to ferment for about half the usual time—in cool fall weather, probably about a week. What really sets this apart is the Asian pear, which stays crispy in the brine and adds an ever-so-slightly sweet contrast to the salty brine and savory ingredients. Because of the pear, I think this goes especially well alongside roasted fall and winter vegetables, but it's great wherever you typically enjoy kimchi.

INGREDIENTS

120 grams Korean radish, cut into ½x½-inch squares, about ⅛ inch thick

150 grams napa cabbage, cut into 1-inch squares

120 grams Asian pear, cut into ½x½-inch squares, about ⅛ inch thick

1 clove garlic, smashed with the back of a knife

1 coin of ginger, no need to peel, cut ⅛ inch thick

Enough 5 percent brine to cover by at least 1 inch

MATERIALS

Basic fermenting supplies

NOTE: As you are cutting the produce for this kimchi, save the Asian pear for last. That way, it goes from the cutting board to the brine as quickly as possible to avoid browning.

Yield: 1 quart

1. In a large nonreactive bowl, use your hands to stir together the radish, napa cabbage, and Asian pear.

2. Place the garlic and ginger in the bottom of a clean quart mason jar.

3. Place the radish, napa cabbage, and Asian pear mixture in the jar on top of the garlic and ginger. You can shake the jar from side to side to help the contents settle in. It should reach just to below the jar's shoulder.

4. Top with enough 5 percent brine so that the produce is fully submerged. Use your hand to gently push down the contents of the jar once or twice to help release air bubbles.

5. Unless your airlock system has a weight built in, weight the contents so that the vegetables remain below the brine. Secure the jar with a mason jar airlock system and allow the kimchi to ferment for up to 8 days. You may begin tasting for doneness after 3 days.

6. Cover, label, and refrigerate for long-term storage.

THE BIGGER THE BETTER IN BRINING

As a general rule, when brining, stick to bigger pieces and whole spices. For example, choose whole garlic cloves crushed with the back of a knife and ginger cut into coins and always place them at the bottom of your jar so they're naturally weighted down by the produce. Ground and crushed spices and very tiny pieces of produce prove harder to weight down in a brine. Because the goal of a ferment is to keep everything submerged to avoid yeast and mold, tiny pieces of organic matter bobbing around in your brine means you're more likely to develop surface yeasts or mold. It's not the end of the world, but it's more work for you. It means more skimming and a higher probability of developing surface yeast.

INGREDIENTS

215 grams parsnips sliced into
1/16-inch-thick coins with a food
processor or mandoline or as thin
as you can with a knife

500 grams turnips, sliced into
1/16-inch-thick coins with a food
processor or mandoline or as thin
as you can with a knife

25 grams ginger, grated but not
peeled

10 grams minced garlic

15 grams salt

12 grams salt-free *gochugaru*
Korean chili flakes

MATERIALS

Basic fermenting supplies
(see page 128)

Mandoline or food processor
(optional)

━━━━ *Yield: 1 scant quart* ━━━━

1. In a large nonreactive bowl, combine the parsnips, turnips, ginger, garlic, and salt. Reserve the gochugaru for now.

2. Use your hands to stir the ingredients together, then work the salt into the produce using your hands for about 2 minutes. If you've ever massaged kale for a salad, that's the motion you want to employ here. In slightly less technical terms, it's basically smooshing. The vegetables will begin releasing their liquid.

3. Use a wooden spoon to stir in the gochugaru.

4. Use your hands to pack the produce tightly into a quart mason jar, one handful at a time.

5. Once the produce is packed into the jar, push it down with your fist, the back of a wooden spoon, or both, a few times.

6. Now the produce should be just covered with its own brine.

7. Secure the jar with a mason jar airlock system and allow the kimchi to ferment for up to 2 weeks. Begin tasting for doneness after 3 days.

8. Cover, label, and refrigerate for long-term storage.

'SNIPS CHI

AN ANSWER FOR WHAT TO DO WITH YOUR WINTER ROOT VEGETABLES BESIDES ROASTING THEM

One winter when I lived in Queens, I was grateful for the opportunity to participate in a winter CSA. It consisted of four or five deliveries throughout the season of about 15 pounds at a time of assorted root vegetables grown on Long Island. I have a particularly vivid memory of one of the deliveries including a turnip the size of my head. Although the standard protocol for this sort of glut of winter root veggies is roasting—and roast I did—I've also come to love the character that they bring to ferments.

Unlike cabbage, which I don't have to tell you makes an irresistible kimchi but doesn't have a particularly strong flavor on its own, this combination of turnips and parsnips has a sweet, nutty, and spicy flavor that really shines through in the finished product. The traditional kimchi spices of *gochugaru*, ginger, and garlic give this all the mouthwatering umami of a cabbage-based kimchi, with the added complexity of the 'snips. Plus, it's a nice option for something other than roasting all those dead-of-winter roots.

fermented JALAPEÑO SLICES

AN INFINITELY VERSATILE BRINE-PICKLED PEPPER

I initially thought I would have a hotter hot sauce in the book, something with habaneros or scotch bonnets. However, I realized there are already plenty of fermented habanero hot sauce recipes out there. Plus, making a hot sauce with jalapeños means two recipes in one: these fermented jalapeño slices, which are ridiculously addictive on their own, can be blended into a fermented hot sauce.

Now, I'm particularly sensitive to the capsaicin in peppers, but I recommend wearing gloves when you're dealing with this many jalapeños—the thick sort of rubber gloves typically used for cleaning or washing dishes. I have a pair that I refer to as my "jalapeño gloves," whose sole purpose is to protect my hands when I'm cutting hot peppers. It's not necessary to seed the jalapeños, but if you want to keep things more mild, you can seed the peppers before fermenting them by slicing them in half lengthwise, scraping out the seeds with your gloved hands, then slicing them and proceeding with the recipe. I probably don't have to tell you that you need these on your nachos, stat.

INGREDIENTS

340 grams jalapeño slices; you can decide how thick you'd like them

Enough 5 percent brine to cover by at least 1 inch

MATERIALS

Basic fermenting supplies (see page 128)

Yield: 1 scant quart

1. Drop the jalapeño slices into a clean quart mason jar, shaking the jar side to side to help them settle, but not packing them down. If you slice them especially thick, you may not fit the full amount in the jar. Fill the jar only to its shoulder.

2. Pour the brine into the jar so that it completely covers the jalapeños. Jiggle a wooden chopstick around in the jar to help remove air bubbles.

3. Weight the contents, secure with an airlock, and allow the jalapeños to ferment for up to 2 weeks. You may begin tasting for doneness after 3 days. Jalapeños and other hot peppers have a tendency to produce more surface yeasts than other vegetables, so if that happens, don't be alarmed; just skim it off and proceed with fermentation.

4. Cover, label, and refrigerate.

INGREDIENTS

Any amount of Fermented Jalapeño Slices (page 144), brine drained

Splash raw apple cider vinegar

MATERIALS

Food processor

Pint or smaller mason jar with 2-piece lid closure

Yield: variable

1. Place the jalapeño slices in a food processor or blender.

2. Add a splash of raw apple cider vinegar—a bigger splash for more slices, a smaller splash for less.

3. Process the slices until they're smooth. The mixture will not be completely uniform if your slices had seeds, but that's OK.

4. Store in a mason jar with 2-piece closure lid in the fridge. Shake well before using.

fermented JALAPEÑO HOT SAUCE

A RUSTIC FERMENTED GREEN PEPPER SAUCE

I'm always interested in hearing about people's hot-sauce brand loyalties. I've witnessed these sorts of conversations reach a level of tension typically reserved for cutthroat sports rivalries and awkward political discussions. I'm one of those rare birds who can go a number of ways depending on what I'm eating, but after I tried a lacto-fermented hot sauce from Hawthorne Valley Farm in New York's Hudson Valley, I was forever changed. It was hot, sour, salty—basically all flavors that I want in a condiment. It took a while before I tried recreating it on my own, but when I finally did, I couldn't get enough.

I kept the yield variable here because all that's really involved in this recipe is puréeing fermented jalapeños. Usually, when I make a batch of the Fermented Jalapeño Slices on page 144, I'll reserve half to be eaten as slices and make half into sauce. It's a big enough batch that it allows for both. If you leave the seeds in for your slices, you can leave the seeds in for the sauce. Unlike a lot of hot sauce recipes, I skip the straining step for a more rustic, spoonable texture.

whole BRINED LEMONS

AN ALMOST-NO-EFFORT METHOD OF SALT PRESERVING LEMONS

Preserved lemons are one of my all-time favorite ingredients. With roots in India and North Africa, lemons preserved in salt are a low-effort, high-payoff way to put up a large amount of lemons at once. Simply cut, salt, and wait. They're unbelievably versatile. I usually make a batch around January or February each year when citrus is in season, then use them in greens, grain salads, and relishes for the rest of the year.

They're a staple in my kitchen and always will be, but when I learned of this Russian variation from canning matriarch Linda Ziedrich, which preserves whole lemons in a salty brine, I was happy to have another salty lemon recipe to add to my repertoire. This recipe is the definition of small batch: depending on the size of your lemons and your jar, you'll likely only fit two or three in a batch. These are fantastic as an addition to relish or salsa but make for especially beautiful presentation when thinly sliced and added to anything from a sandwich to roast chicken. Note that this recipe doesn't use a typical 5 percent brine.

INGREDIENTS

2 to 3 Meyer lemons

3 cups water

41 grams salt

1 sprig fresh rosemary

MATERIALS

Basic fermenting equipment (see page 128)

Yield: 2 to 3 preserved lemons

1. Place the lemons in a clean quart mason jar. Depending on the size of your lemons, you'll likely fit only 2, maybe 3, in a quart jar. Do not pack them. Add the rosemary sprigs to the jar.

2. In a glass bowl or another quart mason jar, combine the water and salt. Stir or shake until the salt is dissolved.

3. Pour the brine into the jar with the lemons, covering them generously.

4. Weighting this ferment is a bit tricky because we want to put a 2-piece lid on it and stash it in the fridge, rather than securing it with an airlock. However, the lemons will float and definitely still need something to keep them submerged. I used a shot glass placed on its side, but this is really a whatever-you-have-that-works type of situation. It needs to be small enough to fit in the jar but still keep the lemons submerged.

5. Cover the lemons and place in the fridge for at least 3 weeks before using.

GOCHUGARU *preserved* LEMONS

INGREDIENTS
6 to 8 lemons, depending on the size of your lemons

Salt

Salt-free *gochugaru*

MATERIALS
1 wide-mouth quart jar

Yield: 1 quart

A CROSS-CULTURAL CITRUS UMAMI PARTY

Gochugaru is the Korean chili pepper flake that provides the notorious bright-red color and signature spice to kimchi. Often ground a little finer than the roasted red pepper flakes we're used to shaking on pizza and a little coarser than ground cayenne, gochugaru has a fruity, complex heat that makes it an ideal foil for preserved lemons. It's important to seek out salt-free gochugaru, as many commercially available brands come premixed with salt.

Because of their shared ability to make just about anything better, it only makes sense to marry these two workhorses of the fermentation world. We're keeping all the best parts of preserved lemons here—they're easy, low effort, versatile, and affordable—and simply adding the mouthwatering heat of kimchi. I've made these with both the more precious, thin-skinned Meyer lemons and big, gangly backyard lemons that show up in shopping bags on my doorstep throughout winter here in Arizona. Because you'll be eating the skin, please do try to seek out organic, unsprayed, or backyard citrus.

1. Trim off the stem end and bottom of each lemon.

2. Set the lemon on its now-flat end and make 3 cuts to slice each one into sixths, stopping about three-fourths of the way down so that the slices do not completely separate the lemon.

3. Add a heaping tablespoon of salt to a wide-mouth quart mason jar.

4. One at a time, holding a cut lemon over the opening of the same wide-mouth quart jar, use a tablespoon to scoop and pour salt between the slices of the lemon, letting the extra fall into the jar. (See illustration on page 151.) Do not worry about leveling the tablespoon perfectly.

5. Then scoop about ½ teaspoon of gochugaru into the lemon in the same way.

6. Push the lemon into the jar however it best fits, hard enough to release its juices. It's OK to smash them in pretty hard.

7. Repeat with the remaining lemons until the jar is full to its shoulder.

8. Top off the jar with another heaping tablespoon of salt, cover the jar with a 2-piece mason jar lid, and allow the jar to sit at room temperature for 24 hours.

9. If after 24 hours the lemons are not comfortably submerged in their own juices, squeeze the juice of an additional 1 to 2 lemons into the jar until they are.

10. Shake the jar and allow it to sit at room temperature for 48 more hours.

11. After 72 hours total, shake the jar and transfer it to the refrigerator for 3 weeks.

12. To serve, remove your desired amount of lemon and mince finely, removing and discarding the seeds as you go. Some people will either rinse the preserved lemons before using or only use the peel, but I like to use them as is and simply adjust the amount of salt in the dish overall.

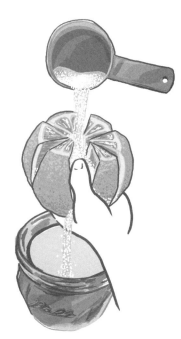

INGREDIENTS

340 grams green cabbage, finely shredded

230 grams daikon, sliced ⅛ inch thick

140 grams brussels sprouts

Zest of 1 lemon

11 grams salt

MATERIALS

Basic fermenting supplies (see page 128)

Yield: 1 scant quart

1. In a large, nonreactive bowl, combine the cabbage, daikon, brussels sprouts, lemon zest, and salt.

2. Use your hands to stir the ingredients together, then work the salt into the produce using your hands for about 2 minutes. If you've ever massaged kale for a salad, that's the motion you want to employ here. In slightly less technical terms, it's basically smooshing. The vegetables will begin releasing their liquid.

3. Use your hands to pack the produce tightly into a quart mason jar, one handful at a time.

4. Once the produce is packed into the jar, push it down with your fist, the back of a wooden spoon, or both, a few times.

5. Now the produce should be just covered with its own brine.

6. Secure the jar with a mason jar airlock system and allow the mixture to ferment for up to 2 weeks. You may begin tasting for doneness after 3 days.

7. Cover, label, and refrigerate for long-term storage.

lemony
SPROUTS
KRAUT-CHI

HOW BRUSSELS SPROUTS WORK BEST IN A FERMENT (FEATURING LEMON ZEST)

Cabbage ferments so consistently and so well that sometimes I'm convinced there's almost nothing that it can't do. It came as a surprise to me, then, that although cabbage, a true workhorse in ferments, is a member of the *Brassica* family, other *Brassicas* have quite different personalities and can result in more finicky ferments. For example, I tried a number of iterations of fermented broccoli while developing recipes for this book, and none of them made the cut.

Because I just love eating them so much, I wanted to incorporate some more *Brassicas* into my ferments. After I found myself eating roasted brussels sprouts with lemon zest for lunch three days in a row, I was inspired to solve my *Brassica* kraut conundrum with—you guessed it— lemon zest and brussels sprouts. The base here is our reliable green cabbage and daikon so things stay pleasantly sour and just funky enough. The lemon zest gives this kraut-chi another layer of sour flavor and complements the sprouts perfectly.

brined
WATERMELON
RADISHES

A THINLY SLICED RADISH PICKLE FOR THE DEPTHS OF WINTER

The first CSA I ever joined would politely call the vegetables that they knew everyone would think were weird "challenge vegetables." So in the e-mail that came from the farm to CSA members preceding each week's delivery, there was a lot of excited chirping about greens and tomatoes, maybe even a watermelon if we were lucky, then a tone shift and the phrase, "This week's challenge vegetable is . . . *cardoons*." Gauntlet thrown.

I consider watermelon radishes a challenge vegetable too. Indeed, they're tasty and beautiful in salads, but in the dead of winter, salads aren't always what I'm craving. I do, however, find myself reaching for a side of tart, nourishing fermented veggies with just about every meal in the cooler months. To preserve the gorgeous color of the watermelon radishes as much as possible, I kept this ferment simple. Most of the radishes' color will transfer to the brine as they ferment, but this is still one of the prettiest ferments around.

INGREDIENTS

400 grams watermelon radishes, sliced 1/16 inch thick on a mandoline or as thin as you can with a knife

Enough 5 percent brine to cover by at least 1 inch

MATERIALS

Basic fermenting supplies (see page 128)

Mandoline or food processor for slicing (optional)

Yield: 1 quart

1. Add the sliced radishes to a quart mason jar, packing them down until they come just to the shoulder of the jar.

2. Pour in the brine so that the radish slices are just covered. Once the brine is added, use your hands to push down on the radishes a couple of times to help release air bubbles.

3. Unless your airlock system has a weight built in, weight the contents so that the vegetables remain below the brine. Secure the jar with an airlock and allow the radishes to ferment for up to 2 weeks. You may begin tasting for doneness after 3 days.

4. Cover, label, and refrigerate for long-term storage.

INGREDIENTS

750 grams (about 2 large) rutabagas, grated

10 grams wakame

12 grams salt

MATERIALS

Basic fermenting supplies (see page 128)

Box grater or food processor

Yield: about 1 scant quart

1. In a large glass bowl, combine the rutabaga, wakame, and salt.

2. Use your hands to stir the ingredients together, then work the salt into the shredded rutabaga using your hands for about 2 minutes. If you've ever massaged kale for a salad, that's the motion you want to employ here. In slightly less technical terms, it's basically smooshing. The rutabaga should begin releasing its liquid quite quickly.

3. Use your hands to pack the rutabaga tightly into a quart mason jar, one handful at a time.

4. Once the rutabaga is packed into the jar, push it down with your fist, the back of a wooden spoon, or both, a few times.

5. Now the mixture should be just covered with its own brine.

6. Secure the jar with an airlock system and allow the mixture to ferment for up to 2 weeks. You may begin tasting for doneness after 3 days.

7. Cover, label, and refrigerate for long-term storage.

RUTABAGA & WAKAME SAUERRUBEN

FEATURING A NUTRIENT-RICH SEAWEED ADD-IN

Sauerruben, as the name suggests, is quite similar to sauerkraut, except that it is typically made with either turnips, rutabagas, or a combination of the two. It's a sauerkraut for the dark days of winter, when fresh cabbage is long gone from the farmer's market. I was so pleasantly surprised the first time I fermented rutabaga. It produces ample brine when dry salted, it gets off to a swift start fermenting right away, and its slightly spicy flavor really shines in the finished ferment. I like having a recipe in my arsenal that quickly dispatches with two or three gnarly rutabagas, so I keep sauerruben a rutabaga-only affair.

Seaweeds are another delicious and nourishing add-in for ferments. Wakame is a mild, slightly sweet seaweed that you'll typically find floating in miso soup. It adds chewy texture to this sauerruben, a bit of green, ocean-y flavor without being fishy. I get my wakame from Mountain Rose Herbs, where it is responsibly sourced and comes prechopped very fine, which I find super convenient for ferments. However, if you purchase wakame in larger pieces, chop it up to about the size of oregano flakes before adding it to the sauerruben.

lime
CURTIDO

THE TRADITIONAL SALVADORIAN KRAUT WITH BRIGHT LIME FLAVOR

The vast majority of *curtido* recipes online ignore this slaw's history as a fermented food and market it as a strictly vinegar-based pickle. Although I love a good pickle as much as the next girl, the misclassification completely ignores this traditional Salvadorian contribution to the kraut canon. Curtido is commonly served alongside *pupusas*, thick tortillas stuffed with cheese, meat, or beans.

Although this ferment starts with green cabbage, carrots have an equally starring role. The carrots' sweetness is the perfect foil for the spicy jalapeños. Plain old white onions, which don't often show up in ferments, are a surprise standout here. Their flavor mellows as they ferment, almost like it would in a sauté, while maintaining a crisp, raw texture. I will almost always pass on raw onions, but these are something else entirely, and I find myself craving their flavor often. I've read of some curtido recipes that include lime juice, but this one includes the zest because I love the bright, concentrated citrus flavor that zest brings to fermented foods.

INGREDIENTS

510 grams green cabbage, shredded

115 grams carrots, thinly sliced

85 grams white onion, thinly sliced

Zest of 1 lime

12 grams salt

30 grams jalapeño, thinly sliced

MATERIALS

Basic fermenting supplies (see page 128)

NOTE: For a more mild curtido, seed the jalapeño.

Yield: 1 scant quart

1. In a large nonreactive bowl, combine the cabbage, carrots, onion, lime zest, and salt. Reserve the jalapeños for now.

2. Work the salt into the vegetables using your hands for about 2 minutes. If you've ever massaged kale for a salad, that's the motion you want to employ here. In slightly less technical terms, it's basically smooshing. The vegetables should begin releasing their liquid.

3. Use a wooden spoon to stir the jalapeños into the shredded vegetable mixture.

4. Use your hands to pack the curtido tightly into a quart mason jar, a handful at a time.

5. Once all the curtido is packed into the jar, push it down with your fist, the back of a wooden spoon, or both, a few times. Now the curtido should be just covered with its own brine.

6. Now, wash your hands! You don't want jalapeño hands.

7. Secure the jar with an airlock and allow to ferment for up to 2 weeks. Begin tasting for doneness after 3 days.

8. Cover, label, and refrigerate for long-term storage.

INGREDIENTS

630 grams cauliflower, thinly sliced on a mandoline or food processor or sliced as thin as possible with a knife

125 grams daikon, grated

11 grams salt

5 grams finely minced garlic

1 gram chipotle powder

MATERIALS

Basic fermentation supplies (see page 128)

Mandoline or food processor (optional)

NOTE: In the process of slicing the cauliflower thin, you're likely to end up with a lot of little pieces of floret breaking off, more like a very coarse meal. You can make use of the little pieces as well. Part of what is nice about using a food processor to shred the cauliflower is that it does a nice job of containing all the small pieces of cauliflower.

Yield: 1 scant quart

1. In a large nonreactive bowl, combine the cauliflower, daikon, and salt.

2. Use your hands to stir the vegetables and salt together, then work the salt into them using your hands for about 2 minutes. If you've ever massaged kale for a salad, that's the motion you want to employ here. In slightly less technical terms, it's basically smooshing. The vegetables should begin releasing their liquid.

3. Let them sit while you mince the garlic, or longer if needed. The cauliflower will take longer to release its liquid than most other veggies, but the daikon helps make up for that.

4. Use a wooden spoon to stir the chipotle and garlic into the shredded vegetable mixture.

5. Use your hands to pack the kraut tightly into a quart mason jar, a handful at a time.

6. Once all the kraut is packed into the jar, push it down with your fist, the back of a wooden spoon, or both, a few times. Now the kraut should be just covered with its own brine.

7. Secure the airlock on top of the jar and allow to ferment for up to 2 weeks. You may begin tasting for doneness after 3 days.

8. Cover, label, and refrigerate for long-term storage.

chipotle-
CAULIFLOWER
KRAUT

A KRAUT WITH A DEEP, SMOKY HEAT (AND HOW TO FIX A DRY FERMENT)

Along with cabbage, cauliflower is a member of the *Brassica* family that takes particularly well to fermentation. Slicing it thin is key, however, so if you don't have a mandoline or a food processor (my preferred method) just go as thin as you can with your sharpest knife. In my experience, cauliflower is one of the few veggies that may not produce adequate brine to fully cover itself when packed into a jar. To address this, I add just a bit of grated daikon. The grated daikon completely blends into the final product—you won't know it's there. More importantly, it lets out a lot of liquid fast, giving the cauliflower a briny boost. In general, remedy any dry kraut or kimchi by adding 100 grams or so of grated daikon and adjusting the amount of salt accordingly.

Taking a cue from recipes like cauliflower steak and roasted cauliflower that use caramelization to amp up flavor in this relatively bland vegetable, we'll use chipotle powder to give this kraut smoky depth.

daikon GARLIC "NOODLES"

FERMENTED VEGETABLE "NOODLES" AND A TEMPLATE FOR OTHER SPIRALIZED FERMENTED VEGGIES

I can be a little wary of social media and was certainly a late adopter, but I'll be the first to admit that I love Instagram. This recipe is a quintessential example of how I often get inspired via Instagram by the creative things other people are eating and making. Case in point: one day Alexa Weitzman, who blogs at sustainablepantry.com, posted what she called "carrot and daikon kimchi noodles." She hadn't given hers a full ferment, but as soon as I saw her picture, a lightbulb went off in my head and I knew I needed a recipe for fermented veggie "noodles."

I wanted to keep these versatile, so they're generously flavored with garlic. The result is a sour, tangy, pungent radish noodle that can be used in a variety of ways. I particularly like mixing them into my lunch salads for an all-vegetable "pasta" salad. Use this recipe as a starting point to experiment with spiralizing and fermenting other roots such as turnips.

INGREDIENTS

715 grams daikon "noodles," cut using the smallest (⅛-inch) spiralizer blade

5 grams minced garlic

11 grams salt

MATERIALS

Basic fermenting supplies (see page 128)

Spiralizer or similar spiral cutter

Yield: 1 scant quart

1. In a large nonreactive bowl, combine the daikon, garlic, and salt.

2. Use your hands to stir the vegetables and salt together, then work the salt into them using your hands for about 2 minutes. You want to be a bit more gentle with this ferment in order to keep the noodles intact. If you've ever massaged kale for a salad, that's the motion you want to employ here. The daikon should readily begin releasing its liquid.

3. Use your hands to pack the noodles tightly into a quart mason jar, a handful at a time. Once all the daikon is packed into the jar, push it down with your fist, the back of a wooden spoon, or both, a few times. Now it should be just covered with its own brine.

4. Secure the airlock on top of the jar and allow to ferment for up to 2 weeks. Begin tasting for doneness after 3 days.

5. Cover, label, and refrigerate for long-term storage.

INGREDIENTS

750 grams baby bok choy, washed, leaves separated, and cut into ½-inch chunks

12 grams salt

10 grams fresh ginger, grated

10 grams garlic, finely minced

12 grams *gochugaru* (Korean chili flakes)

MATERIALS

Basic fermenting supplies (see page 128)

Yield: 1 scant quart

1. Combine the baby bok choy and salt in a large nonreactive bowl.

2. Use your hands to stir everything together, then work the salt into the vegetables for about 2 minutes. If you've ever massaged kale for a salad, that's the motion you want to employ here. In slightly less technical terms, it's basically smooshing. The vegetables should begin releasing a liquid.

3. Use a wooden spoon to stir in the ginger, garlic, and gochugaru.

4. Use your hands to pack the mixture tightly into a quart mason jar, a handful at a time.

5. Once all the mixture is packed into the jar, push it down with your fist, the back of a wooden spoon, or both, a few times. Now it should be just covered with its own brine.

6. Secure the airlock on top of the jar and allow to ferment for up to 2 weeks. Begin tasting for doneness after 3 days.

7. Cover, label, and refrigerate for long-term storage.

TAKE IT SLOWLY

For water-bath canning, I advocate having your tools and ingredients all set up in advance. This helps manage the elements of timing involved in that type of preserving. Fermentation, however, is quite different. I actually find it more beneficial not to have a *mise en place* (all the ingredients prepped and ready) when beginning a fermentation project. In recipes like this baby bok choy kimchi, for example, that use larger pieces of produce that may not release their water as readily, I like to build time into a recipe by combining the veggies and salt and letting them sit while I prep the remaining ingredients. This ensures that there's ample brine when it comes time to pack the vegetables into the jar.

BABY *bok choy* KIMCHI

A STRAIGHTFORWARD KIMCHI WITH A BOK-CHOY BASE

When I was coming up with recipes for this book, I tried to think about those CSA vegetables that threw me for a bit of a loop. I usually get so excited about new-to-me or oddball ingredients (those "challenge vegetables"), that the more mundane stuff—the veggies I saw week after week—were more often what led me to ask, "What am I going to do with this?" For me, baby bok choy is one of those vegetables.

This is my basic, highly untraditional kimchi recipe. I don't typically use green onions or scallions in my kimchis, as a nod to the fact that they're not always in season. I also omit fish sauce to keep the recipes vegetarian friendly.

This recipe dispatches with a quite sizable amount of baby bok choy. One of the great things about measuring by weight is that if the amount of baby bok choy you have falls short of the necessary 750 grams, you can make up the extra weight by supplementing with what you have on hand—thinly sliced carrots, thinly sliced daikon or other radish, napa cabbage, or turnips would all be nice.

kumquat KIMCHI

A NAPA CABBAGE KIMCHI WITH AN UNEXPECTEDLY DELICIOUS ADDITION

Like the Tomato-Vanilla Jam in the sweet preserves chapter, this is a bit of a trust-me-on-this recipe. I love salt-preserved citrus, and I also love the way citrus works as an add-in for vegetable ferments, which is why I included it in so many of the recipes in this chapter. The proven track record of citrus and ferments and some serious fridge serendipity (in less romantic terms, napa cabbage and kumquats jammed in the same crisper drawer) were the inspiration for this recipe.

This unlikely pairing works because a good *gochugaru* will have bright, citrusy notes that really complement and amp up citrus flavor. The ginger is also a great foil for the kumquats. The kumquat skins provide a nice bit of chew and textural interest in the finished product. Finally, as if kimchi weren't flavor-packed enough, sweet-tart kumquats provide serious umami. I left the garlic out of this kimchi because I think it makes less sense flavorwise with the kumquats. However, if garlic in kimchi is a nonnegotiable for you, please feel free to leave it in.

INGREDIENTS

550 grams napa cabbage, cut into ½-inch chunks

10 grams salt

100 grams kumquats, cut into eighths

15 grams ginger, grated

12 grams *gochugaru* (Korean chili flakes)

MATERIALS:

Basic fermenting supplies (see page 128)

=== *Yield: 1 scant quart* ===

1. Combine the napa cabbage and salt in a large nonreactive bowl.

2. Use your hands to stir the cabbage and salt together, then work the salt into the cabbage for about 2 minutes. If you've ever massaged kale for a salad, that's the motion you want to employ here. In slightly less technical terms, it's basically smooshing. The cabbage should begin releasing a liquid.

3. Use a wooden spoon to stir in the ginger, kumquats, and gochugaru.

4. Use your hands to pack the mixture tightly into a quart mason jar, a handful at a time.

5. Once all the mixture is packed into the jar, push it down with your fist, the back of a wooden spoon, or both, a few times. Now it should be just covered with its own brine.

6. Secure the airlock on top of the jar and allow to ferment for up to 2 weeks. You may tasting for doneness after 3 days.

7. Cover, label, and refrigerate for long term storage.

NOTE: In my experience, this ferment is another particularly active one, so keep a close eye on it around day 3 to be sure it doesn't clog the airlock.

spring onion & RED-RADISH-CUBE KIMCHI

INGREDIENTS

460 grams red radishes cut into ½-inch cubes; depending on the size quartering them should work

9 grams salt

150 grams spring onion bulbs and green tops

6 grams *gochugaru* (Korean chili flakes)

MATERIALS

Basic fermenting supplies (see page 128)

— *Yield: 1 scant quart* —

1. In a large nonreactive bowl, use your hands to stir the radishes and salt together, then work the salt into them using your hands for about 2 minutes. If you've ever massaged kale for a salad, that's the motion you want to employ here. In slightly less technical terms, it's basically smooshing. The radishes should just begin to feel wet.

2. Cover the radishes and let them sit at room temperature for 1 hour.

3. In the meantime, slice the spring onion greens into 1-inch pieces.

4. Remove the roots from the onion bulbs and cut each bulb in half vertically, so that you can peel apart the layers. Set aside the prepped onion.

5. After 1 hour, or when the radishes have released ample liquid, use a wooden spoon to stir in the onion and chili flakes.

6. Use your hands to pack the mixture tightly into a quart mason jar, a handful at a time. You can really press this one, as the cubes can take some effort to pack in.

7. Once all the mixture is packed into the jar, push it down with your fist, the back of a wooden spoon, or both, a few times. Now it should be just covered with its own brine.

8. Secure the airlock on top of the jar and allow to ferment for up to 2 weeks. You may begin tasting for doneness after 3 days.

9. Cover, label, and refrigerate for long-term storage.

FEATURING SPRING VEGETABLES WITH A CUBED TEXTURE INSPIRED BY *KKAKDUGI*

Although fall and winter veggies are often the standbys when it comes to kimchis and krauts, this recipe is proof that there are plenty of candidates for delicious ferments at the early-spring greenmarket. Inspired by *kkakdugi*, a Korean kimchi traditionally made with daikon radish cubes, this version uses cubed red radishes and square-cut spring onions and their greens. The bite of the onions and garlic combine with the Korean chili flakes for a layered, spicy condiment.

Because the radish cubes have less surface area than thinly sliced or grated radishes, they won't release their liquid as readily, so they get a bit of a head start in this ferment. Mix them together with the salt first and let them sit for up to 1 hour, until they produce ample brine. You'll wait to mix the onions in until right before packing the mixture into the jar, because onions can make for a slightly slimy brine when massaged with salt. The sliminess will go away as the ferment matures, but it can be a bit unpleasant nonetheless and is easily avoided.

HOW TO PREP SPRING ONIONS FOR SPRING ONION & RED-RADISH-CUBE KIMCHI

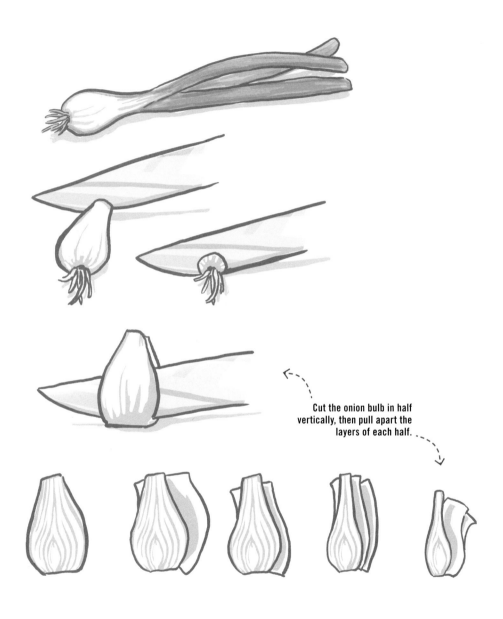

Cut the onion bulb in half vertically, then pull apart the layers of each half.

INGREDIENTS

6 hard-boiled eggs

¼ cup mayonnaise

¼ cup Chow-Chow Kraut, finely chopped (see page 172)

1½ teaspoons Chow-Chow Kraut brine

¼ teaspoon sriracha

Salt and pepper to taste

— *Yield: 12 deviled eggs; recipe can easily be doubled* —

1. Peel the hard-boiled eggs, cut them in half lengthwise, and pop out their yolks into a medium bowl.

2. Add the mayonnaise, chopped kraut, brine, and sriracha to the yolks, and use a fork to smash the ingredients together until smooth. Taste the filling, then add salt and pepper to taste. It's likely you won't need to add additional salt beyond what's in the brine, so do taste it first.

3. Scoop 1 tablespoon of filling into each of the hollowed-out whites.

4. Refrigerate until ready to serve.

chow-chow KRAUT DEVILED EGGS

THE CLASSIC PICNIC FOOD WITH JUST ENOUGH FUNKY, FERMENTED FLAVOR

Eggs and kraut became a favorite breakfast of mine as I was writing this book and always had plenty of kraut on hand. Usually the eggs were fried or scrambled, just out of ease, but when I realized how great a combo eggs and kraut were, I was eager to find more ways to put them together.

While you could experiment with any of the fermented vegetables in this chapter, the Chow-Chow Kraut (page 172) is a good starting point because it functions a lot like pickle relish. Providing tang, crunch, and just the right amount of salt, it makes a ton of sense in deviled eggs. In addition, adding a bit of brine to the yolk mixture provides the filling with both the necessary salt and a complex, briny flavor. Even if you're not a spice person, I'd urge you not to omit the sriracha. It adds just the slightest amount of heat and flavor that really pulls everything together.

CHOW-CHOW KRAUT

INGREDIENTS

375 grams green cabbage, shredded

100 grams red bell pepper, cut into 2-inch matchsticks

250 grams cauliflower, thinly sliced using a food processor or mandoline, or sliced as thinly as possible with a knife

11 grams salt

5 grams finely minced garlic

⅛ teaspoon turmeric

¼ teaspoon crushed red pepper

¼ teaspoon celery seed

MATERIALS

Basic fermenting supplies (see page 128)

Yield: 1 scant quart

A FAVORITE CATCH-ALL VINEGAR PICKLE RELISH THAT WAS BEGGING TO BE FERMENTED

As you now know from the last section, chow-chow is a hodgepodge pickle relish, often quite sweet and distinguished by its yellow color and mustardy flavor. It's also a water-bath canning mainstay that lends itself to fermentation really well. I was inspired to first make this kraut after I realized how much I love cauliflower in ferments. The intention behind chow-chow—making the most of the last of the garden—has so much in common with the spirit of many vegetable ferments that I couldn't help but bring the two together.

I made a few key departures from the bulk of chow-chow recipes. First, I opted out of the mustard seeds and powder. Whereas mustard is typically dominant in many traditional chow-chow recipes, I really wanted the sour veggies to provide the star flavor here. I also used garlic instead of the typical onion because I thought it had the potential to be even more delicious. And I think I was right! The result is a funky, no-sugar version of the classic relish.

1. In a large nonreactive bowl, combine the cabbage, bell pepper, cauliflower, and salt.

2. Use your hands to stir everything together, then work the salt into the vegetables for about 2 minutes. If you've ever massaged kale for a salad, that's the motion you want to employ here. In slightly less technical terms, it's basically smooshing. The vegetables should begin releasing their liquid.

3. Stir in the garlic, turmeric, crushed red pepper, and celery seeds using a wooden spoon.

4. Use your hands to pack the mixture tightly into a quart mason jar, one handful at a time.

5. Once all the mixture is packed into the jar, push it down with your fist, the back of a wooden spoon, or both, a few times. Now it should be just covered with its own brine.

6. Secure the airlock on top of the jar and allow to ferment for up to 2 weeks. You may begin tasting for doneness after 3 days.

7. Cover, label, and refrigerate for long-term storage.

INGREDIENTS

805 grams green cabbage, shredded

12 grams salt

10 juniper berries, crushed with the back of a knife and finely chopped

1 tablespoon fresh grapefruit zest, from one small grapefruit

MATERIALS

Basic fermenting supplies (see page 128)

Microplane or other fine zester to zest the grapefruit

Yield: 1 scant quart

1. In a large nonreactive bowl, combine the cabbage, salt, juniper berries, and grapefruit zest.

2. Use your hands to stir everything together, then work the salt into the mixture for about 2 minutes. If you've ever massaged kale for a salad, that's the motion you want to employ here. In slightly less technical terms, it's basically smooshing.

3. Use your hands to pack the mixture tightly into a quart mason jar, a handful at a time.

4. Once all the mixture is packed into the jar, push it down with your fist, the back of a wooden spoon, or both, a few times. Now it should be just covered with its own brine.

5. Secure the airlock on top of the jar and allow to ferment for up to 2 weeks. You may begin tasting for doneness after 3 days.

6. Cover, label, and refrigerate for long-term storage.

salty-dog KRAUT

A KRAUT INSPIRED BY A FAVORITE COCKTAIL THAT USES FRESH, GRATED PEELS FOR CONCENTRATED FLAVOR

Some cocktail-inspired krauts might be a bit of a hard sell. I can't imagine I'd appreciate a tequila sunrise kraut. However, the salty dog—a simple combination of grapefruit juice, gin, and salt—was the blueprint for this kraut, and once you try it, I won't have to convince you that it really works.

Juniper berries are traditional ingredients in both krauts and gin. When I've added them whole to krauts in the past, I've found their flavor overwhelming when I encounter one every few bites. So, for this recipe, we smash them with the back of a knife and finely chop them first, just as you would with garlic. This doubles as a way to test if the berries are fresh—they'll retain some softness and smash easily with the back of a knife if they are. The grapefruit zest provides vibrant, concentrated fresh-grapefruit flavor that intensifies as the kraut develops.

pink-salt KRAUT

A STRAIGHTFORWARD BASIC KRAUT RECIPE WITH MINERAL-RICH HIMALAYAN PINK SALT

Some folks swear by Himalayan pink salt for all of their ferments. It has a reputation for being pure, mineral rich, and beneficial in a number of ways. I won't argue with any of that. There's one big reason I don't ferment with it on a regular basis and didn't make a requirement for the ferments in this book: it's significantly more costly than sea salt. Seeking out fine-grain Himalayan pink salt in the bulk bins and buying a few tablespoons, however, is an easy and affordable way to experiment with this high-quality salt in ferments.

Because I was interested in exploring the salt, I chose a completely straightforward sauerkraut recipe. It's funny that changing just one variable—salt—made me aware of all the other variables—place, time of year, amount of rain, and so on—that have the potential to influence the final result of a ferment. I'm sure you'll have fun comparing the flavor of this kraut to the other krauts that come out of your kitchen.

INGREDIENTS

800 grams green cabbage, shredded

12 grams Himalayan pink salt

MATERIALS

Basic fermenting supplies (see page 128)

Yield: 1 scant quart

1. In a large nonreactive bowl, combine the cabbage and salt.

2. Use your hands to stir them together, then work the salt into the cabbage for about 2 minutes. If you've ever massaged kale for a salad, that's the motion you want to employ here. In slightly less technical terms, it's basically smooshing.

3. Use your hands to pack the mixture tightly into a quart mason jar, a handful at a time.

4. Once all the mixture is packed into the jar, push it down with your fist, the back of a wooden spoon, or both, a few times. Now it should be just covered with its own brine.

5. Secure the airlock on top of the jar and allow to ferment for up to 2 weeks. You may begin tasting for doneness after 3 days.

6. Cover, label, and refrigerate for long-term storage.

INGREDIENTS

550 grams radicchio, roughly chopped into ½-inch pieces

200 grams sunchokes, scrubbed and sliced 1/16 inch thick on a mandoline, or as thin as you can with a knife

1 heaping teaspoon fresh thyme

11 grams salt

MATERIALS

Basic fermenting supplies (see page 128)

Mandoline or food processor for slicing (optional)

Yield: 1 scant quart

1. In a large nonreactive bowl, combine the radicchio, sunchokes, thyme, and salt.

2. Use your hands to stir everything together, then work the salt into the vegetables for about 2 minutes. If you've ever massaged kale for a salad, that's the motion you want to employ here. In slightly less technical terms, it's basically smooshing. The vegetables should begin releasing a murky-looking liquid. Don't worry; the final color of the kraut is a vibrant magenta.

3. Use your hands to pack the mixture tightly into a quart mason jar, a handful at a time.

4. Once all the mixture is packed into the jar, push it down with your fist, the back of a wooden spoon, or both, a few times. Now it should be just covered with its own brine.

5. Secure the airlock on top of the jar and allow to ferment for up to 2 weeks. Begin tasting for doneness after 3 days. The top portion of this kraut will oxidize slightly as it develops. It's harmless and will go away once the top layer is pushed under the brine again.

6. Cover, label, and refrigerate for long-term storage.

NOTE: Because sunchokes can be knobby, it's important to look for dirt in their nooks and crannies. I don't peel them unless their skin is particularly rough and I suspect they're harboring hidden dirt. Another note about this ferment: In my experience, it is *incredibly* active around days 2 and 3. I had it climb and clog the airlock when it was most active. Around these most active times, you may need to push the contents down quite frequently or take some out to enjoy.

radicchio & sunchoke KRAUT WITH THYME

A SQUARE-CUT KRAUT WITH BITTER GREENS AS A BASE

I love bitter flavors and am always interested in incorporating them into ferments, but bitter greens such as dandelion don't make a good foundation for krauts because their texture doesn't hold up well. Enter radicchio. For a long time, perhaps because it's so beautiful, I loved looking at radicchio but didn't quite know what to do with it. I'd guess I'm not the only one in this predicament.

I'm here to tell you that fermentation does wonders to transform radicchio, which, even for a bitter fiend like me, can be a bit intense—it mellows slightly, without losing its bite. Plus, cutting it with the sweet, nutty sunchokes adds both crunch and balance. Because bitter flavors do wonders for digestion, I particularly like this kraut alongside a rich meal or accompanying a meat or cheese plate as a digestif.

brined GREEN TOMATOES WITH BASIL

INGREDIENTS

1 garlic clove, crushed with the back of a knife

1 fresh basil sprig, about 4 leaves

425 grams green or very underripe tomatoes, cut into sixths

Enough 5 percent brine to cover by at least 1 inch

MATERIALS

Basic fermenting supplies (see page 128)

Yield: 1 scant quart

1. Place the crushed garlic clove and the basil at the bottom of a quart jar.

2. On top of the garlic and basil, add the tomato pieces, 1 handful at a time. You can shake the jar from side to side to help them settle, but do not pack them down. They should come no higher than the top of the jar's shoulder.

3. Pour the brine into the jar so it completely covers the vegetables. Use a wooden chopstick to jiggle the contents to help remove air bubbles. Weight, cover with an airlock, and ferment for up to two weeks. You may begin tasting for doneness after 3 days.

4. Cover, label, and refrigerate for long-term storage.

A FRESH, HERB-INFUSED BRINE PERFECT FOR TOMATOES (AND HOW TO STORE BRINED VEGGIES THAT USE FRESH HERBS)

The degree of ripeness greatly affects how tomatoes behave in a ferment. Some folks like to ferment whole, ripe cherry tomatoes, which transform into something often known as cherry bombs due to their effervescent, explosive quality. Here, we're using green or significantly underripe tomatoes. Using these firmer tomatoes means that they can be sliced and brined without fear of their turning to mush. Plus, they maintain a nice bit of crunch, even when they're fully fermented.

In general, less is more when it comes to fresh herbs in ferments. Their flavor will amplify as it infuses the brine throughout the fermentation period. Likewise, for long-term storage, it can be a good idea to pick out the herbs. If you're eating them regularly and tasting, it may not be necessary to pick them out initially, but do so if and when the flavor of the herb becomes overpowering. The same can be true for the garlic.

KOHLRABI SPEARS

INGREDIENTS

400 grams peeled kohlrabi, sliced into ¼-inch-thick spears

Enough 5 percent brine to cover by at least 1 inch

MATERIALS

Basic fermenting supplies (see page 128)

Yield: 1 scant quart

1. Place the kohlrabi spears in a quart jar. You can shake the jar from side to side to help them settle, but do not pack them down. They should come no higher than the top of the jar's shoulder.

2. Pour the brine into the jar so it completely covers the vegetables. Use a wooden chopstick to jiggle the contents to help remove air bubbles. Weight, cover with an airlock, and allow to ferment for up to 2 weeks. You may begin tasting for doneness after 3 days.

3. Cover, label, and refrigerate for long-term storage.

A CRUNCHY, BRINED LATE-SEASON PICKLE

My mom always had kohlrabi in our garden when I was growing up, and it probably won't surprise you to learn that I wasn't always as big a fan of it as I am now. I commonly snuck into the garden to raid the sweet snap pea vines and ate a dirt-covered carrot or two in my day, but the kohlrabi were safe. My sister and I referred to them as "alien spaceships," and when they showed up on the table we weren't excited. Our recoil from kohlrabi had nothing to do with its taste and everything to do with the fact that it looked like something from another planet.

Now, I know that kohlrabi is a crisp, refreshingly mild member of—surprise—the *Brassica* family. The bulb part of the kohlrabi that we commonly eat is botanically a stem, rather than a root or bulb. The leaves are edible too. Save for one variety that is meant to grow very large, avoid any more than 4 or so inches across, as they can be fibrous and woody. Kohlrabi are one of the few vegetables that I peel before fermenting because the skin can also be fibrous. This crunchy-crisp pickle is perfect for when you want something cool and fresh-tasting, but cucumbers are no longer in the greenmarkets.

fermented CARROT & DAIKON MATCHSTICKS

THE CLASSIC BÁNH MÌ ACCOMPANIMENT, BRINED

One of the first women to turn me on to preserving was Audra, from the blog Doris and Jilly Cook. A recipe of hers also turned me on to the idea of fermenting carrots and daikon together. Seasonal partners, carrots and daikon can usually be found in markets in both the late fall and very early spring, after carrots have been overwintered. Beyond showing up in greenmarkets at around the same time, they're also found together in the iconic slaw on the popular Vietnamese sandwich bánh mì.

Rather than pickling with vinegar, as would be traditional, we're fermenting the carrot and daikon matchsticks for extra umami. This recipe is great for beginners because it's simple, ferments for a short time, and isn't finicky at all. Your food processor or mandoline with a matchstick blade would be the perfect choice here. Otherwise, some quality time with your sharpest knife will do just fine. Although inspired by the Vietnamese sandwich condiment, this slaw can be enjoyed with just about anything: alongside eggs or grain salads and even on nachos!

INGREDIENTS
175 grams carrot matchsticks

175 grams daikon matchsticks

Enough 5 percent brine to cover

MATERIALS
Basic fermenting supplies (see page 128)

Mandoline with matchstick blade or food processor (optional)

Yield: 1 scant quart

1. In a large, nonreactive glass bowl, use your hands to stir together the carrots and daikon.

2. Use your hands to transfer the matchsticks to a quart mason jar. You can shake the jar from side to side to help the vegetables settle.

3. Pour the brine over the vegetables. Use a wooden chopstick to jiggle the contents to help remove air bubbles and adjust the level of brine if needed.

4. Unless your airlock has a built-in weight, weight the vegetables to keep them submerged and cover with an airlock.

5. Let ferment at room temperature for up to 2 weeks. You may begin tasting for doneness after 3 days.

6. Cover, label, and refrigerate for long-term storage.

ACKNOWLEDGMENTS

To my mom, thank you for always telling me I could do it, making the sacrifices so that I could, and for somehow knowing that the best way to support a daughter who is writing a book on the other side of the country is to send leggings and chocolate.

I still can't believe how much I lucked out to have an editor like Thom O'Hearn. Thank you for taking a risk on me and giving me the space to write the best book I could. I couldn't have asked for a kinder, smarter, more supportive editor.

To my agent, Judy Linden, thank you for talking me down when I needed it and being my biggest advocate. I'm so grateful to have you on my team.

I have armloads of gratitude for Grace Stufkosky, for her immense talent and eye for light that made the recipes in this book look better than I ever could have imagined. Go, Grace, go!

I'm deeply thankful for fellow preservers Kate Payne, Julia Sforza, Kaela Porter, Marisa McClellan, Sean Timberlake, Shae Irving, and Kate Boucher for inspiration, leadership, and friendship. Thanks especially to Kaela Porter for being a shine theory role model.

Kelly Vass is always my biggest cheerleader, and I appreciate it so much. Thank you also for texting me cat pictures at just the right times.

Casey Barber's advice was hugely important to me in the early stages of working on this book. Thank you, Casey!

To Tiéra Guereña and Katie Gardea, thank you for still coming over even though our house was a disaster and smelled like sauerkraut while I worked on this book.

Thank you Zoë, Sam, and Nathan Sterk for the beautiful citrus deliveries, and Diana and Bob Tunis for all the dinners, jars, and rides to Phoenix.

To Molly Cornwell and Johnu Brown at the White Porch in Globe, Arizona, thank you for many of the props that helped make the recipes shine and for not hesitating to sell me the pretty jar you were using to hold your pens. It's in the book! Thank you also to Hill Street Mall in Globe, Arizona, for many beautiful props.

To Marc Marin, thanks for being the sort of boss who will do his employee's job for her while she finishes her canning book. You're one of a kind.

I am forever indebted to Namita Tolia for giving me four years of a day job that was actually a day job, which is perhaps the greatest gift a freelancer-on-the-side in New York City can ever receive. I value your generosity and friendship and truly wouldn't be here without you.

To my sister, Kelsey Giles, thank you for knowing the power of a well-timed hair-flip emoji text and always making sure I was breathing.

Finally, to Paul, thank you for telling me you were proud of me until you were sure that I heard it. I feel so grateful to have you.

ABOUT THE AUTHOR

Autumn Giles is a freelance writer and recipe developer whose work has appeared in *Modern Farmer*, *New American Homesteader*, *PUNCH*, *Serious Eats*, *Edible Baja Arizona*, and elsewhere. She has an MFA in poetry from Sarah Lawrence College and a BA in English from Barnard College. Autumn grew up in Montana and, after spending ten years in New York City, now lives in an old pink house in rural Arizona with two gray cats and Paul Tunis, the book's illustrator. She blogs at autumnmakesanddoes.com and is on Twitter and Instagram @autumnmakes.

Photo credit: Tiéra Guereña

RESOURCES

PRODUCTS
NIELSEN-MASSEY
www.nielsenmassey.com
Although they're known for their superb vanilla extracts and beans, Nielsen-Massey makes a particularly high-quality rosewater that can be a game changer, even for folks who might think they don't like the floral add-in.

MIGHTYNEST
www.mightynest.com
MightyNest is an online retailer that I rely on for glassware such as nesting bowls for macerating fruit and Weck jars. The Duralex picardie tumblers pictured throughout the book are also from MightyNest.

FARMCURIOUS
www.farmcurious.com
A successful Kickstarter project, FARMcurious sells a high-quality small-batch fermentation setup, the FARMcurious Fermenting Set, which uses the reCAP mason jar pouring lid, a BPA-free top for any wide-mouth mason jar that has a spout for easy pouring. I like this because if it's not in use for fermentation, you can use the reCAP for other things, like shaking, pouring, and storing homemade dressing right in the jar.

BALL
www.freshpreserving.com
Ball is the gold standard for canning jars in the United States and also maintains a sizable searchable recipe collection online.

OXO

www.oxo.com

I can't stress enough how much easier a good cherry pitter, strawberry huller, and other processing tools will make your preserving life. OXO is my trusted source for this sort of equipment.

LEMON LADIES ORCHARD

www.lemonladies.com

If you don't have Meyer lemons available to you locally, the Lemon Ladies Orchard in California ships fragrant, unsprayed Meyer lemons all over the world. I've ordered from them a number of times, and there's really nothing better than opening a box full of beautiful Meyer lemons in the middle of winter.

LOCAL HARVEST

www.localharvest.org

Use Local Harvest to support small producers and purchase produce that may not be available to you locally. I've used Local Harvest in the past to purchase organic kumquats and limes and have them delivered to my door.

MOTHER-IN-LAW'S KIMCHI (MILK)

www.milkimchi.com

MILK is my favorite brand of commercially available kimchi. Luckily, they sell their salt-free, high-quality *gochugaru* blend online and it's all I use.

ACE HARDWARE

www.acehardware.com

When I lived in NYC, I frequently took advantage of Ace Hardware's option to buy online and get free pickup at my local Ace in order to buy jars.

FILLMORE CONTAINER

www.fillmorecontainer.com

Fillmore Container is a Pennsylvania-based online retailer that has just about every type of jar and closure imaginable.

KRAUT SOURCE

www.krautsource.com

This Cadillac of small-batch fermentation setups was originally a Kickstarter project that is now available to purchase online. Its stainless steel construction and built-in weighting mechanism sets it apart from other similar systems out there. Plus, I'm totally enamored with the little chirp it makes when gas escapes. It's a worthwhile investment.

MOUNTAIN ROSE HERBS

www.mountainroseherbs.com

Mountain Rose Herbs is my favorite online source for high-quality, bulk, organic herbs and spices. I get ingredients like wakame, hibiscus, and pink peppercorns from this site.

WEBSITES

PUNK DOMESTICS

www.punkdomestics.com

Run by Sean Timberlake, Punk Domestics is an online preserving community, recipe aggregator, and fantastic source of information on a wide breadth of preserving techniques and projects. Timberlake is also the force behind About.com's Food Preservation content at www.foodpreservation.about.com, which is another great resource.

NATIONAL CENTER FOR HOME FOOD PRESERVATION

nchfp.uga.edu

Based out of the University of Georgia, the National Center for Home Food Preservation sets the standard for home food preservation. Their website offers self-study courses, recipes, and more.

OSU LANE COUNTY EXTENSION

www.extension.oregonstate.edu/lane/food-preservation/publications

A number of county extension offices around the country make information available online, but I've found Lane County's to be one of the most extensive. They have an impressive number of food preservation publications available on a wide variety of preserving topics, all available to download for free.

FOOD IN JARS

www.foodinjars.com

The popular preserving blog created by Marisa McClellan is a place for recipes, information on the newest canning products and accessories, and more.

HITCHHIKING TO HEAVEN

www.hitchhikingtoheaven.com

Created by California-based preserver Shae Irving, Hitchhiking to Heaven is a collection of creative recipes that shows a deep appreciation for ingredients.

LOCAL KITCHEN

www.localkitchenblog.com

Kaela Porter is the Hudson Valley–based blogger behind the site Local Kitchen. In addition to practical recipes and tips for seasonal eating, Kaela's site is an invaluable source of preserving recipes.

THE PRESERVED LIFE

www.thepreservedlife.wordpress.com

Julia Sforza is a preserving educator and owner of the Good Food Award–winning Half Pint Preserves. Her site, the Preserved Life, which chronicles her everyday eating and preserving, is a constant inspiration.

THE HIP GIRL'S GUIDE TO HOMEMAKING

www.hipgirlshome.com

At the Hip Girl's Guide to Homemaking, Kate Payne shares small-batch preserving recipes plus tips for reducing food waste and maintaining a harmonious home.

BOOKS

The Art of Fermentation, Sandor Ellix Katz

Ball Blue Book Guide to Preserving, Ball Fresh Preserving Kitchen

Fermented Vegetables, Kirsten K. Shockey and Christopher Shockey

The Joy of Pickling and *The Joy of Jams, Jellies, and Other Sweet Preserves*, Linda Ziedrich

Mes Confitures: The Jams and Jellies of Christine Ferber, Christine Ferber

Mrs. Wheelbarrow's Practical Pantry, Cathy Barrow

Preserving by the Pint, Marisa McClellan

Preserving for a New Generation, Liana Krissoff

Put 'Em Up and *Put 'Em Up Fruit*, Sherri Brooks Vinton

Saving the Season, Kevin West

USDA Complete Guide to Home Canning and Preserving, US Department of Agriculture

Well-Preserved, Eugenia Bone

INDEX